Praise for *LEFT TO TELL*

"I am humbled by the extraordinary spirituality that shines throughout Immaculée Ilibagiza's story of terror, endurance, healing, and forgiveness. As a Rwandan, I am proud that we can look beyond the misconceived differences that resulted in the murder of so many of our children, men, and women in 1994. Immaculée's account of genocide survival is truly astonishing. It gives us hope of overcoming the divisions deliberately created by those with self-serving agendas and no thought for humanity. Everyone should read this story—survivors as well as perpetrators. I hope that all can experience Immaculée's profound spiritual transformation and be inspired to work for a united and lasting nation."

— **Jeannette Kagame,** First Lady of the Republic of Rwanda

"Into a confused world that has lost its moral compass comes Immaculée Iligabiza's book, offering luminous direction, and pointing us straight toward the path of reconciliation. As the horrific acts of the Rwandan genocide escalate, Immaculée's faith deepens. It is this unsettling tension between horror and faith that haunted me long after my tears and nausea had subsided. Although the details of Immaculée's story are unique, what is profoundly universal is the way her belief in goodness is tested over and over. As unspeakable evil spreads around her, and she has to dig deeper and deeper to find compassion, hope, and ultimately the kind of genuine forgiveness that offers redemption. **Left to Tell** *will leave you breathless and falling to your knees with renewed faith."*

— **Gail Straub,** director, The Empowerment Institute;
the author of *The Rhythm of Compassion*

"We all ask ourselves what we would do if faced with the kind of terror and loss that Immaculée Ilibagiza faced during the genocide in her country. Would we allow fear and desperation to fill us with hatred or despair? And should we survive, would our spirit be poisoned, or would we be able to rise from the ashes still encouraged to fulfill our purpose in life, still able to give and receive love? In the tradition of Viktor Frankl and Anne Frank, Immaculée is living proof that human beings can not only withstand evil, but can also find courage in crisis, and faith in the most hopeless of situations. She gives us the strength to find wisdom and grace during our own challenging times."

— **Elizabeth Lesser,** co-founder of the Omega Institute, and
author of *Broken Open: How Difficult Times Can Help Us Grow*

LEFT TO TELL

HAY HOUSE TITLES OF RELATED INTEREST

Ask and It Is Given: Learning to Manifest Your Desires,
by Esther and Jerry Hicks (The Teachings of Abraham)

An Attitude of Gratitude: 21 Life Lessons, by Keith Harrell

Count Your Blessings: The Healing Power of Gratitude and Love,
by Dr. John F. Demartini

The End of Karma: 40 Days to Perfect Peace,
Tranquility, and Bliss, by Dharma Singh Khalsa, M.D.

The God Code: The Secret of Our Past, the Promise of Our Future,
by Gregg Braden

Gratitude: A Way of Life, by Louise L. Hay and Friends

If I Can Forgive, So Can You: My Autobiography
of How I Overcame My Past and Healed My Life,
by Denise Linn

In Real Life: Powerful Lessons from Everyday Living,
edited by Karl Zinsmeister, with Karina Rollins

Inspiration: Your Ultimate Calling, by Dr. Wayne W. Dyer

Miracles, by Stuart Wilde

Never Mind Success . . . Go for Greatness!
The Best Advice I've Ever Received, as told to Tavis Smiley

The Power of Intention: Learning to Co-create
Your World Your Way, by Dr. Wayne W. Dyer

➤➤◄◄

All of the above are available at your local bookstore,
or may be ordered by visiting:

Hay House USA: **www.hayhouse.com**®
Hay House Australia: **www.hayhouse.com.au**
Hay House UK: **www.hayhouse.co.uk**
Hay House South Africa: **orders@psdprom.co.za**

LEFT TO TELL

Discovering God
Amidst the Rwandan Holocaust

Immaculée Ilibagiza

with Steve Erwin

HAY HOUSE, INC.
Carlsbad, California
London • Sydney • Johannesburg
Vancouver • Hong Kong

Published and distributed in the United States by: Hay House, Inc., P.O. Box 5100, Carlsbad, CA 92018-5100 • *Phone:* (760) 431-7695 or (800) 654-5126 • *Fax:* (760) 431-6948 or (800) 650-5115 • www.hayhouse.com • *Published and distributed in Australia by:* Hay House Australia Pty. Ltd., 18/36 Ralph St., Alexandria NSW 2015 • *Phone:* 612-9669-4299 • *Fax:* 612-9669-4144 • www.hayhouse.com.au • *Published and distributed in the United Kingdom by:* Hay House UK, Ltd. • Unit 62, Canalot Studios • 222 Kensal Rd., London W10 5BN • *Phone:* 44-20-8962-1230 • *Fax:* 44-20-8962-1239 • www.hayhouse.co.uk • *Published and distributed in the Republic of South Africa by:* Hay House SA (Pty), Ltd., P.O. Box 990, Witkoppen 2068 • *Phone/Fax:* 27-11-706-6612 • orders@psdprom.co.za • *Distributed in Canada by:* Raincoast • 9050 Shaughnessy St., Vancouver, B.C. V6P 6E5 • *Phone:* (604) 323-7100 • *Fax:* (604) 323-2600

Editorial supervision: Jill Kramer • *Design:* Tricia Breidenthal
Interior photos courtesy of the author

Library of Congress Cataloging-in-Publication Data

Ilibagiza, Immaculée.
  Left to tell : discovering God amidst the Rwandan holocaust / Immaculée Ilibagiza, with Steve Erwin.
    p. cm.
  ISBN-13: 978-1-4019-0896-6 (hardcover)
  ISBN-10: 1-4019-0896-9 (hardcover)
  ISBN-13: 978-1-4019-0897-3 (tradepaper)
  ISBN-10: 1-4019-0897-7 (tradepaper)
  1. Ilibagiza, Immaculée. 2. Catholics--Rwanda--Biography. 3. Rwanda--History--Civil War, 1994--Personal narratives. I. Erwin, Steve. II. Title.
  BX4705.I46A3 2006
  282.092--dc22

2005031509

  Hardcover: ISBN 13: 978-1-4019-0896-6 • ISBN 10: 1-4019-0896-9
  Tradepaper: ISBN 13: 978-1-4019-0897-3 • ISBN 10: 1-4019-0897-7

09 08 07 06   4 3 2 1
1st printing, February 2006

Printed in the United States of America

*To my beloved parents, Leonard and Rose;
and my dear brothers Damascene and Vianney, for all
the selfless love you gave me. You make heaven
a brighter place, and I will love you always.*

*For my brother Aimable, with much love
and in hopes of healing unspoken pain.*

*And to my new family—Bryan and our sweet babies,
Nikki and Bryan, Jr.—for giving me a new life, love,
and inspiration. You make my life complete.*

In memory of holocaust victims everywhere.

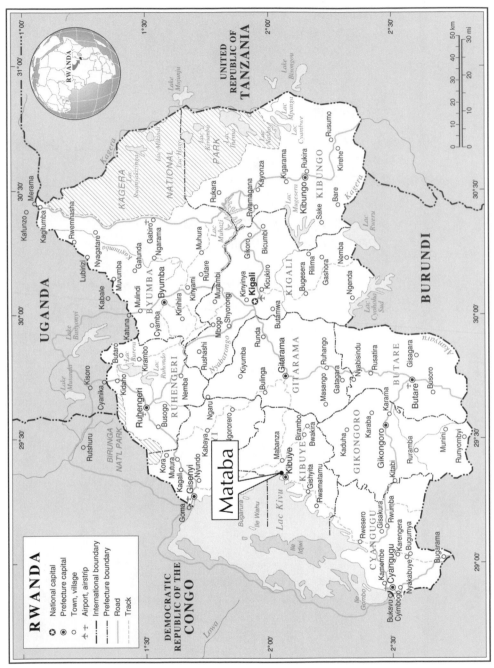

Immaculée's hometown, Mataba, which is north of Kibuye and west of Mabanza, on the shores of Lake Kivu.

CONTENTS

*"When we are no longer able to change a situation—
we are challenged to change ourselves."*

— Viktor E. Frankl, psychologist, author,
and Nazi holocaust survivor

FOREWORD

I've read thousands of books over the past 50 or so years. The book you hold in your hands is by far the most moving and poignantly significant of the vast library that comprises my lifetime of personal reading.

You're about to embark on a journey that will undoubtedly change the way you view the power of faith—forever. A single phrase from the scriptures reminds us that "with God all things are possible." I've quoted this passage frequently in my lectures, often adding the rhetorical question: "Now what does that leave out?" The answer is obvious to all: "All things means all things."

You've read that pure faith, devoid of all doubt, can move mountains and even project a camel through the eye of a needle. But even with your own unshakable faith, the mountain has probably remained stationary where it's always been, and the eye of the needle is too tiny to welcome even one camel's eyelash—let alone the entire creature traversing a minuscule opening. Well, I'm happy to report that when you've completed your first reading of *Left to Tell*, you'll have a new perspective on what the field of *all* possibilities looks like. As you bear witness to Immaculée Ilibagiza's transcendent experience in the midst of a holocaust too horrible to even contemplate, you'll also understand how the limitless power of pure, undeterred faith can indeed work to create miracles.

Despite the hideous display of humans' inhumanity to each other that was taking place only a decade or so ago in the country of Rwanda, this is truly a love story in the purest sense of the word—a story of the triumph of the human spirit, a story of one woman's profound faith and determination to survive (against literally impossible odds) in order to tell her tale and to be an agent for ushering in a new spiritual consciousness, and a story of a love for God that was so strong that hatred and revenge were forced to dissolve in its presence.

I have come to know Immaculée very, very well over the past year—in fact, we communicate on a daily basis. She's traveled with me, speaking on the same stage and telling her story to audiences that number in the thousands. We've talked privately for hour after hour about her experiences in the holocaust and her ambitions today, and I've spent time with her and her family. I've spoken with her co-workers and even her fellow holocaust survivors, and she's spent a great deal of time with my own children. I've conversed with her during long plane and train rides between lecture stops, and I've seen her stand before audiences large and small. I've come to know this dynamic, powerful woman so well that I count her as one of my closest friends. In fact, I've come to love and admire her so much that I've dedicated my latest book, *Inspiration,* to her.

I reveal my own personal relationship with Immaculée here in the opening pages of this extraordinary work because I want you, who are about to be immersed into an experience that will change your life forever (and I believe is destined to change *the world* for the better as well), to know firsthand what a phenomenal human being Immaculée Ilibagiza is in my eyes. In all of my countless hours with her, in this multitude of private and public settings, this transcendentally spiritual woman always—and I mean *always*—shines a light that captures everyone within its boundaries.

When she converses at a dinner table, all who are present not only listen, they're magnetically drawn to her; and in large audiences, you can hear a pin drop as she speaks from her heart with so much conviction. There is something much more than charisma at work here—Immaculée not only writes and speaks about unconditional love and forgiveness, but she radiates it wherever she goes. She lives at an elevated level of spiritual consciousness, and by doing so, she raises the energy level of all those whom she encounters . . . including myself.

The very first moment we met, I knew in an absolute flash of insight that I was in the presence of a uniquely Divine woman (something that will be evident when you complete this book). We briefly spoke after a presentation I made in New York City for the Omega Institute, and after only a second or two, she was gone from my sight—but in those few moments, I was captured. I sensed her exceptionally high energy, similar to the way I felt after having been with Mother Meera (an Indian woman who's thought to be an incarnation of the Divine Mother) many years before.

Immaculée didn't seek me out for assistance in having this book published—*I* was the one who did the seeking. That inner glow of joy and love that I felt in her company wouldn't leave me, so I asked my daughter Skye, who had exchanged e-mail addresses with Immaculée, to please make every effort to contact her. Days turned into weeks, and there was still no communication. Each day I'd ask Skye, "Have you heard from the woman from Rwanda?"

Finally, Immaculée responded to my daughter's inquiries, and I telephoned her immediately. I asked her one question: "Would you be willing to write your story of survival? I feel compelled to help you get the message to the world." It was then that Immaculée told me she herself had already written down every detail of her ordeal as a Tutsi woman in Rwanda who was being hunted and marked for certain death during the genocide of 1994. She told me she felt that this was the reason why she'd been spared, but that her efforts in being published were unsuccessful, largely because English was her third language and she needed help in getting the essence of her story converted to a more readable format.

It was at this point that I asked her to send me everything she'd written, which turned out to be about 150,000 words in which she'd painstakingly recorded every detail some five years after leaving Rwanda. I made one phone call to my friend Reid Tracy, the president of Hay House, and arrangements were made to have writer Steve Erwin help Immaculée tell her story in the way that it's written on these pages. I told Reid that I would support this project in every way possible: Not only would I write the Foreword, but I'd also help bring Immaculée and her story to all of my public appearances. In addition, I'd travel to Rwanda with her and her family and help her raise money to fulfill her mission of aiding the many orphaned children left behind when the killing finally stopped.

In addition, I told Reid that I wanted to include Immaculée in my Public Television special on *Inspiration: Your Ultimate Calling,* and that I'd do everything in my power to bring this spiritual woman's saga to the public eye. And all of this was done because of that feeling I had when I first met her, at the back of a room full of people, for only a few moments.

It has been said that *the laws of the material world do not apply in the presence of the God-realized.* You'll come to understand these words directly by the time you finish reading this book. Time after time, Immaculée's pure, God-realized "Inner Beingness" allowed her to erect invisible barriers so that killers with machetes who were only inches away were blinded to her physical presence. As her faith deepened, the miracles became even more astonishing. Her visualizations became so real—and all doubt was banished from her mind—that she was indeed at one with God. She knew that God was with her as she saw a cross of light bar her and her companions from certain death. Angels of love and compassion seemed to emerge out of nowhere as Immaculée intensified her communion with our Creator. She was able to stare down a determined killer and watch in certainty as he dropped his weapon and became immobilized as his contempt was converted to kindness.

And finally, as she abandoned all of her feelings of hatred and revenge toward the killers—and despite what once seemed an impossibility—she merged into Divine union with God by offering her tormentors not only compassion, but total forgiveness and unconditional love as well. Yes, she became one with Spirit, where she remains today.

Her story will touch you deeply. You will feel her fear, you will cry, and you will ask yourself the same questions that we as a people have been asking forever: *How could this happen? Where does such animosity come from? Why can't we just be like God, Who is the Source for all of us?* But you will also feel something else most profoundly: You will feel hope, a hope that inch by inch, we as a people are moving toward a new alignment—that is, we're moving toward living God-realized lives.

To me, Immaculée was not only left to tell this mind-blowing story, but more than that, she's a living example of what we can all accomplish when we go within and choose to truly live in perfect harmony with our originating Spirit.

I am honored to have played a small role in bringing this staggering story to the attention of the world. I am honored to join hands with Immaculée and assist in her vision of love and compassion—not only in Rwanda, but in all places where hatred has resided for so long. And I am deeply honored to write these few words in this book that you, the reader, are about to immerse yourself in. I assure you that as you do so, you'll move to a place just a few inches closer to living in oneness with the same Divine Essence from which we were all created.

I love this book, and I love Immaculée Ilibagiza.

Immaculée, thank you for coming into my life.

— **Wayne Dyer,** Maui, Hawaii

PREFACE

This book is not intended to be a history of Rwanda or of the genocide; rather, it is my own history. A number of very good, informative books have been published recently exploring in detail the politics and mechanics of the 1994 genocide in which, according to Rwandan government estimates, more than one million people were murdered in roughly 100 days.

This is my story, told as I remember it . . . and I remember it as though it happened yesterday. It's a true story; I use my own name and the names of my family. However, I have changed most of the names of others who appear in the book to protect the identity of the survivors and to avoid perpetuating the cycle of hatred.

I believe that our lives are interconnected, that we're meant to learn from one another's experiences. I wrote this book hoping that others may benefit from my story.

— **Immaculée Ilibagiza**, New York City

INTRODUCTION

My Name Is Immaculée

I heard the killers call my name.

They were on the other side of the wall, and less than an inch of plaster and wood separated us. Their voices were cold, hard, and determined.

"She's here . . . we know she's here somewhere. . . . Find her—find Immaculée."

There were many voices, many killers. I could see them in my mind: my former friends and neighbors, who had always greeted me with love and kindness, moving through the house carrying spears and machetes and calling my name.

"I have killed 399 cockroaches," said one of the killers. "Immaculée will make 400. It's a good number to kill."

I cowered in the corner of our tiny secret bathroom without moving a muscle. Like the seven other women hiding for their lives with me, I held my breath so that the killers wouldn't hear me breathing.

Their voices clawed at my flesh. I felt as if I were lying on a bed of burning coals, like I'd been set on fire. A sweeping wind of pain engulfed my body; a thousand invisible needles ripped into me. I never dreamed that fear could cause such agonizing physical anguish.

I tried to swallow, but my throat closed up. I had no saliva, and my mouth was drier than sand. I closed my eyes and tried to make myself disappear, but their voices grew louder. I knew that they would show no mercy, and my mind echoed with one thought: *If they catch me, they will kill me. If they catch me, they will kill me. If they catch me, they will kill me. . . .*

The killers were just outside the door, and I knew that at any second they were going to find me. I wondered what it would feel like when the machete slashed through my skin and cut deep into my bones. I thought of my brothers and my dear parents, wondering if they were dead or alive and if we would soon be together in heaven.

I put my hands together, clasped my father's rosary, and silently began to pray: *Oh, please, God, please help me. Don't let me die like this, not like this. Don't let these killers find me. You tell us in the Bible that if we ask, we shall receive . . . well, God, I am asking. Please make these killers go away. Please don't let me die in this bathroom. Please, God, please, please, please save me! Save me!*

The killers moved from the house, and we all began to breathe again. They were gone, but they would be back many times over the next three months. I believe that God had spared my life, but I'd learn during the 91 days I spent trembling in fear with seven others in a closet-sized bathroom that being spared is much different from being saved . . . and this lesson forever changed me. It is a lesson that, in the midst of mass murder, taught me how to love those who hated and hunted me—and how to forgive those who slaughtered my family.

My name is Immaculée Ilibagiza. This is the story of how I discovered God during one of history's bloodiest holocausts.

>*<

PART I

THE GATHERING STORM

CHAPTER 1

The Eternal Spring

I was born in paradise.

At least, that's how I felt about my homeland while I was growing up.

Rwanda is a tiny country set like a jewel in central Africa. She is so breathtakingly beautiful that it's impossible not to see the hand of God in her lush, rolling hills; mist-shrouded mountains; green valleys; and sparkling lakes. The gentle breezes drifting down from the hills and through the pine and cedar forests are scented with the sweet aroma of lilies and chrysanthemums. And the weather is so pleasant year-round that the German settlers who arrived in the late 1800s christened her "the land of eternal spring."

The forces of evil that would give birth to a holocaust that set my beloved country awash in a sea of blood were hidden from me as a child. As a young girl, all I knew of the world was the lovely landscape surrounding me, the kindness of my neighbors, and the deep love of my parents and brothers. In our home, racism and prejudice were completely unknown. I wasn't aware that people belonged to different tribes or races, and I didn't even hear the terms *Tutsi* or *Hutu* until I was in school.

In my village, young children walked eight miles to and from school along lonely stretches of road, but parents never worried about a child being abducted or harmed in any way. My biggest fear as a youngster was being alone in the dark—other than that, I was an extremely happy little girl in a happy family, living in what I thought was a happy village where people respected and cared for one another.

I was born in the western Rwandan province of Kibuye, in the village of Mataba. Our house was perched on a hilltop overlooking Lake Kivu, which seemed to stretch out forever below us. On clear mornings I could see the mountains on the other side of the lake in the neighboring country of Zaire, now called the Democratic Republic of the Congo. Some of my warmest childhood memories are of clambering down the perilously steep hill between our house and the lake. I'd go swimming with my dad and brothers as the last of the dawn mist was being chased away by the early-morning sun. The water was warm, the air cool against our skin, and the view of our house high above the shore always thrilling.

Heading back home was an adventure because the hill was so steep and the dirt beneath our feet was so loose and treacherous. I often slipped and was afraid that I'd tumble all the way down and into the lake. My father always knew when I was frightened, and he'd bundle me in his arms all the way home. He was a big, strong man, and I felt safe and loved wrapped in those powerful arms. It thrilled me to be lifted up so affectionately, especially since Dad was very reserved in an old-fashioned way and rarely showed his emotions or said he loved my brothers and me—although we knew he did.

When we got home from our swim, my beautiful mother would be busy in the kitchen preparing the hot rice-and-bean dish she fed us every day before packing us off to school. Her energy never failed to astonish me: Mom was always the first to rise and last to bed, getting up hours before anyone else to make sure that the house was in order, our clothes were laid out, our books and lessons were ready, and my father's work papers were organized. She made all our clothing herself, cut our hair, and brightened the house with handmade decorations.

The beans she prepared for our breakfast were grown in our family fields, which Mom tended every morning while the rest of us were still sleeping. She checked the crops and would then distribute tools to the day laborers and make sure that our cows and other animals were fed and watered. And then, after finishing the morning chores and getting us off to class, Mom would walk down the road to start her full-time teaching job at the local primary school.

Both of my parents were teachers, and adamant believers that the only defense against poverty and hunger was a good education. Despite being one of the smallest countries in Africa, Rwanda—which is roughly the size of the American state of Maryland—is one of the most densely populated countries on the continent and among the poorest in the world. Mom and Dad were the first high school graduates in their families, and they were determined that their children would go even further than they had in school. Dad led by example, working hard and studying throughout his life. He received many honors and promotions during his career, rising steadily through the ranks from primary teacher to junior high school principal. He was eventually appointed chief administrator for all of the Catholic schools in our district.

In Rwanda, every family member has a different last name. Parents give each child a unique surname at birth, one that reflects the feelings of the mother or father at the moment they first lay eyes on their new baby. In Kinyarwanda, the native language of Rwanda, my name (Ilibagiza) means "shining and beautiful in body and soul." My dad chose my name, which will always remind me how much he loved me from the moment I was born.

My father's name was Leonard Ukulikiyinkindi, and my mother's was Marie Rose Kankindi, but her friends called her Rose. They met at one of my cousin's homes in the summer of 1963 while traveling to a mutual friend's wedding. As they were introduced, Mom gave Dad the once-over, clucking her tongue at his shaggy hair.

"You're going to a wedding with that hair?"

My father shrugged, claiming that he couldn't find a barber. Mom found a pair of scissors, sat him down, and went to work—right then and there. She must have done a good job, because they became inseparable. They married within the year, and Dad never let anyone but Mom cut his hair again.

My parents managed to save a little money by holding down teaching jobs and farming the land my grandfather had given them (they grew and sold beans, bananas, and coffee). Dad designed and built our house, which, while extremely modest by Western standards, was considered quite luxurious in our village. We had a kitchen, a dining area, a living room, our own bedrooms, a guest room, and Dad even had a study. A gated courtyard led to a small annex where day workers stayed, and—thankfully—we had a separate pen for the animals, so the cows didn't sleep in the house with us. Dad put a cistern on the roof to catch rainfall so that we wouldn't have to haul water up from Lake Kivu, and the solar panels he installed provided us with about an hour of electricity on sunny days.

We had two vehicles, which was practically unheard of in our part of Rwanda. We had a yellow cross-country motorcycle that Dad used to visit schools in the remote mountain villages, and we also had a little car that we used on weekends to go to church and visit relatives. Some villagers thought that we were wealthy, which we weren't, and they called my Dad *Muzungu,* meaning "white man" or "rich person," which to most Rwandans meant the same thing.

No one else in our village had a motorcycle, and Mom always worried that Dad would be waylaid by bandits on a lonely mountain pass. Fretting about her family was a preoccupation with my mother, to the point that whenever any of us was away from home for more than a night, she'd listen to the obituaries announced on the radio every evening.

"Mom, think of all the good things that could happen to us instead of dwelling on what might go wrong," I urged her unsuccessfully.

"Oh, Immaculée, I couldn't bear it if someone knocked on the door with bad news about one of my children or your father. I just pray that I die before any of you do." She prayed incessantly for our health, safety, and well-being.

My parents were devout Roman Catholics and passed on their beliefs to us. Mass was mandatory on Sundays, as were evening prayers with the family at home. I loved praying, going to church, and everything else to do with God. I especially loved the Virgin Mary, believing that she was my second mom, watching out for me from heaven. I didn't know why, but praying made me feel warm and happy. In fact, it made me so happy that when I was ten years old, I snuck away from school one day with my friend Jeanette to pay a visit to Father Clement, a wise, elderly priest who was a good friend of the family and like a grandpa to me.

Jeanette and I hiked through seven miles of fields and forests and waded across a river to reach Father Clement. He greeted us warmly, but was concerned because we arrived at his presbytery exhausted, panting, soaking wet, and more than a little dirty. He looked like a saint, standing over us in his flowing white robe, his arms opened in welcome, a beautiful rosary hanging from his neck. "What is it, girls? How can I help you?" he asked.

"Father, we want to dedicate our lives to God," Jeanette said solemnly.

"That's right, Father," I agreed. "We have thought it over, and we want to become nuns."

"Nuns? I see," he said, nodding seriously, although I'm sure he must have been hiding a big grin. He placed his hands on our heads and gave us a special blessing: "God, bless these dear children, keep them safe, and watch over them all their days." Then he looked at us and said, "Now, you two go home. Come back to see me after your 18th birthdays, and if you still want to be nuns then, we'll talk."

WHILE MY PARENTS WERE ARDENT CATHOLICS, they were Christians in the broadest sense of the word. They believed in the Golden Rule and taught us to treat our neighbors with kindness and respect. They felt strongly connected to their village and dedicated themselves to creating a prosperous, harmonious community. Dad spent many weekends doing volunteer work, such as building a nondenominational chapel and paying for most of the construction costs out of his own pocket. He also set up a scholarship fund for poorer kids by establishing one of Rwanda's few coffee cooperatives, allowing a dozen coffee growers to plant on his land rent free if they promised to donate a little of their profits to the fund. The program was so successful that he was able to use some of the money to build a community center, a soccer field for teens, and a new roof for the school.

Mom was also known for her many good works. She could never turn away anyone in need, so we often had another family living with us because they'd fallen on hard times and needed a place to stay until they got back on their feet.

After finishing work, my mother often volunteered her time to tutor students, and she was forever buying material to sew new uniforms for local schoolgirls. And once I overheard her talking to a neighbor who was distraught because she couldn't afford to buy her daughter a wedding dress.

"Rose, what kind of mother am I to send my own daughter to her new life in old clothes?" the woman asked. "If only we had a goat to sell, I could dress her in the way she should be dressed on her wedding day."

My mother told her not to worry—if she had faith in God, He would provide. The next day I saw Mom counting out the money she'd saved from her monthly teacher's salary. Then she walked to the village, coming home with her arms full of brightly colored fabrics. She sat up all night sewing dresses for the woman's daughter and all the bridesmaids.

Mom and Dad treated the village as our extended family, and the villagers often treated them like surrogate parents. For example, Dad had a reputation across the region as an educated, enlightened, and fair-minded man. Consequently, people traveled for miles seeking his counsel on family problems, money woes, and business ventures. He was often called upon to settle local squabbles and discipline unruly children.

A crisis in the village was usually followed by a knock on our door and this plea: "Leonard! Can you help us out? We need your advice. What should we do, Leonard?"

Dad invited people into the house at all hours and would discuss their problems until they found a solution. He was a good diplomat and always made people feel as if they'd resolved their own difficulties.

My mother was also sought out for her advice, especially by women having difficulties with their husbands. Over the years, so many of our neighbors had once been Mother's students that most villagers just called her Teacher.

But while they were certainly dedicated to our village, my parents were devoted to their kids, spending as much time with us as possible.

Once in a while, when he worked late and went for beers with his friends afterward, Dad got home well after we'd already gone to bed. "Where are my little ones? Where are my darling children?" he'd ask, a little tipsy but full of affection.

Mother would scold him: "They're sleeping, Leonard, as they should be. If you want to see them, you should come home earlier."

"Well, I can't eat dinner alone," he'd say, and gently get us all out of bed. We'd sit around the table in our pajamas while he ate dinner and told us about his day. We loved every minute of it.

After he finished eating, Dad would make us all kneel down in the living room and recite our evening prayers.

"They've already said their prayers, Leonard. They have school tomorrow!"

"Well, Rose, I have to work tomorrow. And you can never say too many prayers. Right, Immaculée?"

"Yes, Daddy," I'd answer shyly. I idolized my dad and was delighted that he'd ask me such an important question.

Those were magical moments—when my father's stern facade was lifted, his love for us was easy to see.

THERE WERE FOUR KIDS IN THE FAMILY: myself and my three brothers. The eldest was Aimable Ntukanyagwe, who was born in 1965, a year after my parents were married. Even as a child, Aimable was the most serious member of the family. He was so quiet and introspective that we joked he was the family priest. Mom doted on him because he was her firstborn and her favorite, but Aimable was humble, shy, and embarrassed by the extra attention she paid him. He was also sweet-natured and detested violence. When the other boys roughhoused or fought with each other, he would step between them and make the peace.

When Dad was away, Aimable took his place, making sure that we finished our homework, said our evening prayers, and got to bed on time. Then he would stay up late, ensuring that the doors were locked and the house was secure for the night. He seemed so much older than his years, but he was a loving brother to me, never failing to ask about my day, how my studies were going, and if my friends were treating me well. There was a five-year age difference between Aimable and me, which, as kids, made it difficult to get to know each other.

I was only seven when my brother went off to boarding school, and after that, we saw each other only on holidays and special get-togethers. Nevertheless, I developed a terrible stomachache the day he left. Although his school was in a nearby town, as far as I was concerned, my brother was moving to the moon. It was the first time I felt the physical pain of losing someone you love. When my father sat us kids down a few days later to write letters to Aimable, I could think of only two things to say. In large, looping letters, I wrote:

> Dear Aimable,
> I love you, I miss you, I love you, I miss you, I love you, I miss you, I love you, I miss you, I love you, I miss you, I love you, I miss you, I love you, I miss you, I love you, I miss you, I love you, I miss you, I love you, I miss you, I love you, I miss you, I love you, I love you, I love you . . . and I miss you!!!!!
> Love,
> Immaculée
> P.S. I miss you!

My father laughed when he read the letter. "You didn't mention anything about visiting Grandma's house, or how your other brothers are doing, Immaculée. Try writing again with a little more news and a few less 'I love yous' and 'I miss yous.'"

"But that's how I feel, Daddy."

I couldn't understand why he wanted me to love my brother less—and Dad never tired of teasing me about that letter.

Two years after Aimable was born, my other big brother came into the world. His name was Damascene Jean Muhirwa, and he was brilliant, mischievous, funny, generous, unbelievably kind, and irresistibly likable. He made me laugh every day, and he always knew how to stop my tears. Damascene . . . to this day I can't say his name without smiling . . . or crying. He was three years my senior, but I felt as though he were my twin. He was my closest friend; he was my soul mate.

Whenever I was feeling low, Damascene would show up and boost my spirits—like the day I was furious at my mother for making me clean the yard while the boys played soccer. Damascene decided to skip the game, leave his pals, and come help me—wearing a skirt!

"A woman's work is never done," he sang out in a high-pitched voice, picking up a rake and making me laugh until it hurt. He spent all afternoon working with me.

Even if he behaved badly, which wasn't often, things had a way of working out for the best. When he was 12 years old, he secretly "borrowed" Dad's car to teach himself how to drive. Normally, my father would have punished him severely for such an offense, but when he found out, he just hugged Damascene. You see, Dad had been out of town on business when Mom suffered a serious asthma attack. She collapsed onto the floor, semiconscious and barely able to breathe. Damascene hoisted her onto his shoulder, carried her to the car, carefully loaded her onto the backseat, and drove nine miles to the nearest hospital. Mind you, he almost collided with two cows, three goats, and several of our neighbors along the way, but he arrived just in time. The doctor said that Mom would have died if she hadn't gotten to the hospital when she did.

Almost everyone who met Damascene loved him—his easy smile and jovial nature were infectious. He was a class clown but also a brilliant scholar, consistently among the top students in his school—and he went on to become the youngest person in the entire region to earn a master's degree. He studied constantly, but somehow managed to find time to earn a brown belt in karate, become captain of his high school and university basketball teams, and serve as chief altar boy at our church. I cried for a week when he left home for boarding school and felt like I'd never laugh again.

He was the light of my life.

The baby of the family was my little brother, John Marie Vianney Kazeneza, born three years after me. Vianney was a wide-eyed innocent who was lovable but pesky, as all younger brothers are, I suppose. He'd grow up to become a handsome, strapping young man who towered over me, but in my eyes Vianney was always my baby brother—I never stopped feeling like it was my responsibility to look out for him. He was a precious boy who followed me everywhere like a puppy dog. I became so accustomed to his constant companionship that I missed him when he wasn't around pestering me.

I was the third child, and the only girl, which, in a male-dominated society, put extra pressure on me. In Rwandan culture, having a "good name" is everything, and my parents were vigilant in making sure that their only daughter maintained a spotless reputation. They were stricter with me than with my brothers, giving me more household chores and more rigid curfews, selecting my clothes, and approving or disapproving of my friends. My parents pushed me to succeed in school and to develop my mind, but as a young woman in a very conservative society, I was still expected to be seen and not heard.

How ironic that I was the one left to tell our family story.

≫⋘

CHAPTER 2

Standing Up

"Tutsis, stand up!"

Half a dozen chairs scraped backward across the floor as six kids in my fourth-grade class jumped to their feet. I didn't have a clue what was happening, since I'd always attended my mom's schoolhouse. Now that I was ten years old, it was my first day at the school for older kids, and I was confused by the commotion. I'd never seen a teacher take ethnic roll call before.

"*All* Tutsis stand up now!" Buhoro, our teacher, yelled. He was checking off names from a list with a big pencil, then stopped and stared directly at me.

"Immaculée Ilibagiza, you didn't stand up when I said Hutu, you didn't stand up when I said Twa, and you're not standing up now that I've said Tutsi. Why is that?" Buhoro was smiling, but his voice was hard and mean.

"I don't know, Teacher."

"What tribe do you belong to?"

"I don't know, Teacher."

"Are you Hutu or Tutsi?"

"I-I don't know."

"Get out! Get out of this class and don't come back until you know what you are!"

I collected my books and left the room, hanging my head in shame. I didn't know it yet, but I'd just had my first lesson in Rwanda's ethnic divide, and it was a rude awakening.

I ran into the schoolyard and hid behind some bushes to wait for my brother Damascene to finish class. I'd been fighting back tears, but now I cried until my blue uniform was soaked through. I didn't understand what had just happened, and I really wanted to go back to class and ask my best friend, Janet, to explain it to me. She'd stood up when the teacher called out the name Hutu—maybe she'd know why our teacher was so mean to me. But I stayed crouched in the bushes until Damascene found me there, still whimpering.

"Who hurt you, Immaculée?" asked my big brother, with all of the authority of his 13 years. Damascene had always been my greatest defender, ready to go to war if ever anyone slighted me, so I told him what Buhoro had said.

"Buhoro is not a nice man," my brother said, "but don't worry about it. Next time he does the roll call, just do what I do: Stand up with your friends. Stand up when your friend Janet does."

"Janet stood up when he called out Hutu."

"Then stand up when they call out Hutu. If that's what our friends are, then that's what we must be. We're all the same people, aren't we?"

I had no way of knowing then, but Damascene was as clueless as I was about tribalism in Rwanda . . . which was odd, considering that we were among the best-educated kids in the area. Every day after school, my brothers and I were allotted just 90 minutes of free time before being summoned to the living room to do our homework under Mom's supervision. Dad took over an hour before dinner, setting up a classroom-sized blackboard in the middle of the room. He handed out pieces of chalk and grilled us on math, grammar, and geography.

But our parents didn't teach us about our own history. We didn't know that Rwanda was made up of three tribes: a Hutu majority; a Tutsi minority; and a very small number of Twa, a pygmy-like tribe of forest dwellers. We weren't taught that the German colonialists, and the Belgian ones that followed, converted Rwanda's existing social structure—a monarchy that under a Tutsi king had provided Rwanda with centuries of peace and harmony—into a discriminatory, race-based class system. The Belgians favored the minority Tutsi aristocracy and promoted its status as the ruling class; therefore, Tutsis were ensured a better education to better manage the country and generate greater profits for the Belgian overlords. The Belgians introduced an ethnic identity card to more easily distinguish the two tribes, deepening the rift they'd created between Hutu and Tutsi. Those reckless blunders created a lingering resentment among Hutus that helped lay the groundwork for genocide.

When the Tutsis called for greater independence, the Belgians turned against them and, in 1959, encouraged a bloody Hutu revolt, which overthrew the monarchy. More than 100,000 Tutsis were murdered in vengeance killings over the next few years. By the time Belgium pulled out of Rwanda in 1962, a Hutu government was firmly in place, and Tutsis had become second-class citizens, facing persecution, violence, and death at the hands of Hutu extremists. Many tens of thousands died over decades when massacres were common occurrences. While the violence was cyclical, discrimination was ever present. The ethnic identity cards the Hutu government adopted from the days of Belgian rule made the discrimination more blatant, and much easier.

But these were history lessons our parents didn't want my brothers and me to learn, at least not while we were young. They never talked to us about discrimination or killing sprees or ethnic cleansing or racial identity cards—those things weren't part of my youth.

Everyone was welcome in our home, regardless of race, religion, or tribe. To my parents, being Hutu or Tutsi had nothing to do with the kind of person you were. If you were of good character and a kind human being, they greeted you with open arms. But my parents themselves had some horrifying experiences at the hands of Hutu extremists . . . and looking back, I can even vaguely recall one of them.

I was just three years old and didn't understand what was happening, but I remember fire lighting up the night sky as my mother held me tightly in her arms and we ran from our home. It was during the 1973 coup, when many Tutsis were persecuted, driven from their homes, and murdered in the streets. In our region, Hutu extremists were torching Tutsi homes one after another. My entire family stood together looking down at Lake Kivu as the fires leapt up the hill toward us. We fled to a neighbor's, a Hutu and a good friend named Rutakamize. He hid us until the killings and burnings stopped. When we returned home, all we found was a smoldering ruin.

My mother and father rebuilt our house and never discussed what happened, at least not with us children. And even though they'd been targeted in similar anti-Tutsi violence in 1959, I never heard my parents say one disparaging word against Hutus. They were not prejudiced; rather, they believed that evil drove people to do evil things regardless of tribe or race. Mom and Dad ignored the social and political reality they lived in, and instead taught that everyone was born equal. They didn't want their children growing up feeling paranoid or inferior because they were born Tutsi.

SO IT'S NOT DIFFICULT TO SEE WHY I WAS SO CONFOUNDED when my teacher, Buhoro, lashed into me for not knowing my tribe.

Damascene draped his arm around my shoulders that day and walked me home. We both sensed that we'd been touched by something bad, but we didn't know what it was. At dinner that night, I told my father what had happened. He became quiet, and then asked me how long I'd sat crying in the bushes after being ordered from the classroom.

"Almost all day, Daddy."

My father put down his fork and stopped eating—a sure sign he was angry. "I will talk to Buhoro tomorrow," he assured me.

"But, Daddy, what tribe am I?"

"Oh, don't worry about that now. We can discuss that tomorrow, after I talk to your teacher."

I wanted to ask why he wouldn't tell me right then what tribe I belonged to, but we weren't supposed to question our elders. He was my father, and if he was being evasive, I figured that he had good reason. But I was frustrated—I couldn't understand why everyone got so upset when they talked about tribes!

Dad spoke to my teacher the next day, but he didn't tell me what they discussed or what my tribe was, as he'd said he would. I didn't find that out until the following week, when Buhoro held tribal roll call again. My father must have shamed him, because he spoke to me in a much sweeter voice when he summoned me to his desk before roll call.

"Immaculée, stand up when I call out 'Tutsi.'"

I smiled as I walked back to my seat, thinking, *So I'm a Tutsi. Good!* I had no idea what a Tutsi was, but I was proud to be one anyway.

There were so few of us in class that I figured we had to be special—besides, the name sounded cute and was fun to say. But I still couldn't see any real difference between the Tutsi and Hutu tribes. The Twa were pygmies, so their smaller stature made them easy to recognize. But since hardly any Twa came to school, I saw very few of them.

The differences between Tutsis and Hutus were more difficult to spot: Tutsis were supposed to be taller, lighter-skinned, and have narrower noses; while Hutus were shorter, darker, and broad-nosed. But that really wasn't true because Hutus and Tutsis had been marrying each other for centuries, so our gene pools were intermingled. Hutus and Tutsis spoke the same language—Kinyarwanda—and shared the same history. We had virtually the same culture: We sang the same songs, farmed the same land, attended the same churches, and worshiped the same God. We lived in the same villages, on the same streets, and often in the same houses.

Through a child's eyes (or at least through *my* eyes), we all seemed to be getting along. I couldn't begin to count the number of times my Hutu friend Janet and I ate dinner at each other's houses. As a young girl, the only time I was reminded that there were different tribes in Rwanda was when I stood up in class once a week during ethnic roll call. It was an annoyance, but it didn't bother me too much because I had yet to discover the meaning of discrimination.

That is, until I wanted to go to high school.

When I was 15 years old, I finished eighth grade second in my class of 60 students. I had an overall average of 94 percent, just 2 percent lower than the top student—a Tutsi boy—and far ahead of all the other students. It was more than enough to ensure a scholarship and placement in one of the best public high schools in the region. I went home at the end of the term dreaming about my new school uniform and wondering what it would be like to live away from home in a fine school where all the classes were taught in French.

After high school I planned to go to university, and after that, who knew? Maybe I would become a pilot, a professor, or even a psychologist (by this point, I'd pretty much given up my childhood idea of becoming a nun). My parents had taught me that with hard work and determination, even a girl from a little village like Mataba could become someone important.

How was I to know that my ambitions were just a silly girl's dream? I didn't know that those weekly roll calls served a sinister purpose: to segregate Tutsi children as part of a master plan of discrimination known as the "ethnic balance."

This was a plan pushed by Juvenal Habyarimana, the Hutu president who seized power in the 1973 coup. He proclaimed that the government must "balance" the number of school placements and good civil-service jobs to reflect the country's ethnic makeup. Because Rwanda's population was roughly 85 percent Hutu, 14 percent Tutsi, and 1 percent Twa, most jobs and school placements went to Hutus. What the plan really did was keep Tutsis out of high school, university, and well-paying jobs, ensuring their status as second-class citizens.

The true meaning of the ethnic balance was brought home to me a few weeks before I was to start high school. A neighbor dropped by as my family was sitting down to dinner and told us that my name wasn't on the list of scholarship students that had just been posted in the village hall. Despite my top marks, I'd been passed over because I was Tutsi—all the available places had gone to Hutus who'd earned much lower grades. The Tutsi boy who'd had the highest marks was also passed over because of his tribe.

My father pushed his chair away from the table and sat with his eyes tightly closed for the longest time. I knew that my parents couldn't afford to send me to a private school, which would cost ten times more than public high school. Both my older brothers were away studying, and money was tight. Besides, private high schools in Rwanda were terrible compared to the well-funded government-run public schools. The teachers were not as qualified, the curriculum was inferior, and the buildings were ugly and uninviting.

"Don't worry, Immaculée. We'll find another way for you to study," my father finally managed. He excused himself from the table and went to his room without finishing his meal.

"Don't give up hope," my mother said, hugging me. "We'll all pray about this. Now eat your dinner."

After supper I locked myself in my father's study and cried. I'd worked my heart out in school, only to have my dreams of a higher education dashed. I shuddered to think of what was in store for me. I'd seen how single women with no education were treated in my society: They had virtually no rights, no prospects, and no respect. Without even a high school education, I'd have no option other than to wait at home for some man to come and claim me as his wife. My future looked bleak, and I was only 15 years old!

The next morning, my father wasn't at the breakfast table.

"He's trying to work a little miracle," my mother explained. "He's gone to look at some private schools to see if he can get you enrolled."

"But, Mom, it's so expensive, and we can't—"

"Shush," she broke in. "I told you not to give up hope, didn't I?"

It turns out that my father had left before sunrise to sell two of our cows so that he could send me to a private high school. Cows are status symbols in Rwandan culture and extremely valuable—selling one was extravagant; selling two was an invitation to financial ruin. But Dad was determined that I would get an education. He took his cow money, drove three hours south to a newly built private school, and paid my first year's tuition in cash. It was difficult for my father to express emotions, but it was impossible for him to conceal his love for me.

A few weeks later, I was packed and ready to go. Janet hugged me, and we cried and promised to write each other many letters. My mother kissed me over and over, fighting back tears. Vianney, now the last of the kids at home, ran to his room and refused to say good-bye. A lot of the neighbors came out to wave farewell as my father and I drove away. I felt pangs of loss leaving Mataba, but I was anxious to start my new life.

MY NEW SCHOOL LEFT A LOT TO BE DESIRED. The dorm room was tiny, and it had a cement floor and rough cinder-block walls that cried out for a cheery coat of paint. I slept with ten other girls on mattresses crammed so close together, they took up nearly every inch of floor space. There was no running water, so every morning we grabbed buckets and hiked two miles to the nearest stream to fetch what we needed to wash and cook. And I missed my bed and my mom's rice and beans.

However, no matter how hard it was for me to "rough it," I was not going to quit school and ask my parents to bring me home. In fact, when it came time to choose our subjects for the year, I selected the most challenging courses: math and physics. Not only did I want to make Mom and Dad proud, I wanted to prove a point to my brothers. Like typical Rwandan men, they teased me about women belonging in the kitchen, not the classroom. Well, I'd show them!

Two years passed, and I was one of the top students in the school. When the government announced that it was holding a special exam for honor students who wanted to enter public school, I decided to take the test. Deep down inside, I felt that it wouldn't matter if I scored the highest test results in the country—I'd still be passed over because I was Tutsi. Nevertheless, I studied hard and was sure that I'd written an excellent exam, but weeks went by without any word, so I put it out of my mind.

Months later I was home on summer vacation when Damascene bounded into the house, bellowing at the top of his lungs, "Immaculée! Immaculée Ilibagiza! I just saw the list—you passed the exam! You've been accepted at Lycée de Notre Dame d'Afrique. It's one of the best schools in Rwanda, and it's just down the road from my school!"

The family was sitting in the living room and everyone went crazy. I jumped out of my seat, yelling, "Thank God, thank God!" and making the sign of the cross as I did a little victory dance across the floor. My mother had tears in her eyes, and my father shouted, "This is the biggest joy in my life! I have gotten on my knees every day for the past two years and prayed you would get into that school. God has answered my prayers!"

"I guess you must be smart, even if you are a girl." Aimable was laughing, but I could see how happy he was for me.

Damascene was smiling his beautiful smile and was so full of pride that I thought he'd explode.

We had a family party that night, one of our happiest celebrations in a very long time. Lycée was an excellent girls' school where many of the daughters of the country's highest-ranking politicians had attended. Not only would I get the best education available to any young Rwandan, but my parents wouldn't have to struggle with the private-school fees anymore. The only drawback was that the school was far away in the province of Gisenyi. Since it was a four-hour drive from Mataba along perilous roads, this meant that my parents wouldn't be able to visit often. And it was also located in a predominantly Hutu area known for being openly hostile toward Tutsis.

"Don't worry, it's a girls' school," Damascene said. "They have a big fence and lots of guards to keep you safe. And my school is so close that I'll be able to visit you at least once a month."

I LOVED LYCÉE RIGHT AWAY. The buildings were spacious, beautiful, and sparkling clean. The classrooms were brightly painted, and there were colorful flowers planted all around the campus. A high security fence ran around the entire complex, making me feel safe and secure. I was happy, and I knew that my father would be, too, especially when the nuns told us that we'd have to pray together before and after meals.

One of the first friends I made was a Hutu girl named Sarah. We became as close as sisters, and she invited me to meet her family in Kigali, Rwanda's capital city. For a simple village girl like me, that trip to the big city was a real eye-opener—especially when I saw airplanes up close for the first time. Sarah and I went to the airport at night, when the runway shimmered in a fluorescent glow and the landing lights flashed red, white, and green as the huge planes descended from the sky. My jaw dropped open when I heard the roar of those gigantic engines.

"Oh, just look at them!" I exclaimed, as Sarah collapsed into laughter. "Now I think I've seen everything."

Another friend I met on my first day was Clementine, a gorgeous young woman whose smooth skin and beautiful eyes gave her the look of an American magazine model. She marched over to me when she spotted me in the crowd of new students. I was taller than most, but she was at least six feet. We recognized each other as Tutsi by our height.

"How is a pretty Tutsi girl like you going to get along so far north, surrounded by all those unfriendly Hutu faces on the other side of the fence?" Clementine smiled. "We'll have to stick together and look out for one another." We hit it off right away.

Clementine was right about the unfriendly faces. It was difficult to venture beyond the campus walls—whenever I did, I felt the eyes of the local people on me and heard them muttering "Tutsi" in a menacing tone. The priests and nuns who ran the school made sure that the students and local residents never attended the same mass at the local church. We were issued strict orders forbidding us to leave school grounds without a staff escort. It was scary out there, but within the walls of the school I never felt any ethnic discrimination. Teachers never took ethnic roll call, and while most of the girls were Hutu, we loved each other like we were family.

I stuck close to campus, studied hard, and tried to keep myself from feeling homesick. I missed my parents and brothers, and I even pined for Vianney's pestering. Speaking of my baby brother, he sent me a touching and troubling letter a few months after I left home. He wrote that he missed me horribly, was unable to sleep since I'd gone, and that at night he sometimes saw ghosts walking from room to room. When he did, he'd run from the house in terror. The letter tore at my heart—yes, Vianney and I had bickered often at home, but now I realized how much I meant to him. I felt guilty for leaving him alone and promised myself that I'd be a better sister to him.

Damascene was true to his word and visited me once a month. We'd sit together on the grass and talk for hours. He always had good advice for me, especially when it came to studying.

"Pray, Immaculée. Pray before you do your homework and whenever you're preparing for a test or exam. Then study as hard as you can." I did as he said, praying especially hard before math exams, and I continued to excel in school.

When Damascene visited, my girlfriends all demanded to know the identity of the handsome boy I'd been talking with so intently. "That was my big brother Damascene," I'd proudly reply.

"No, it wasn't. Nobody gets along so well with a brother. You looked like you actually *enjoyed* being with him."

I was so lucky to have my dear Damascene in my life.

>*<

CHAPTER 3

Higher Learning

Life was good at Lycée until war broke out in my third and final year.

It was a beautiful sunny afternoon on the first day of October 1990. My classmates and I were waiting for our Civil Education class to begin and wondering why our teacher was late. Mr. Gahigi was an easygoing, friendly man and perhaps the calmest person I'd ever met. So when he finally showed up wringing his hands and pacing back and forth at the front of the classroom, we knew that something was wrong. One of the students asked him what was the matter, but he continued pacing and wouldn't look at us.

I wondered what bad news our teacher was keeping from us, thinking he was probably going to tell us that the nuns had cancelled movie night. But it was something much bigger. We weren't allowed to listen to news broadcasts at school, so just like at home, I was isolated from what was going on in the real world.

"I've just found out that there has been an attack on the country," Mr. Gahigi informed us somberly. "I'm afraid it is very serious and could have an impact on all of us for a long time to come."

The class fell silent—and then everyone started talking at once, shouting out questions, wanting to know who was attacking Rwanda and why.

"A group of Tutsi rebel soldiers living in Uganda has crossed the border," he replied. "They are mainly the children of Rwandan refugees who have banded together and are fighting to get back into the country. There is a lot of fighting going on right now north of here between the rebels and the Rwandan government soldiers."

Mr. Gahigi was bombarded with a volley of frightened and indignant questions: "What do those Tutsis want? Why are they attacking us? What will they do to us if they reach the school?"

I felt the heat of shame on the back of my neck and wanted to crawl under my desk. There were 50 students in the class, and 47 of them were Hutus. I was so nervous and self-conscious that I couldn't look at the other two Tutsi girls. It was the first time I'd felt embarrassed about being Tutsi, and the first time I felt singled out at Lycée.

"The rebels are soldiers fighting with the Rwandese Patriotic Front. That's a political association of Tutsis who left the country years ago and have been forbidden by the government from returning. They're foreigners, really, and they're waging a war to get back into Rwanda and take over the government."

I knew about the Rwandese Patriotic Front, or RPF, and I knew that the people in it weren't fighting simply to topple the Hutu government; they wanted to live in a country that was free and equal. Most of the RPF soldiers—the rebels—were Tutsi exiles or the children of Tutsi exiles.

Hundreds of thousands of Tutsis had fled Rwanda during the troubles of 1959 and 1973, as well as the many other times that Hutu extremists had gone on Tutsi killing sprees. They'd gone into exile to save their lives and those of their families. Mr. Gahigi called the rebels "foreigners" because most of them grew up in neighboring countries such as Uganda and Zaire—but that was only because President Habyarimana enforced a policy banning exiles from ever returning to Rwanda. He'd created a Tutsi diaspora, and entire generations of Rwandan Tutsis had grown up without once setting foot in their homeland.

Mr. Gahigi didn't mention any of that, but he knew what happened whenever Tutsis fought back against extremist Hutus. He was worried for us, saying, "This could go very hard for Tutsis. This kind of thing can lead to many killings, so let's pray that the government and the rebels can settle their differences peacefully and we avoid a lot of bloodshed."

Our class was essentially over. The girls talked of nothing but the attack and what they would do if Tutsi soldiers arrived at the school. I sat quietly with my two Tutsi classmates, trying to be inconspicuous. My shame slowly transformed into anger as I thought about how unfairly Tutsis had been treated. I silently rooted for the RPF, hoping that the rebels would beat the government soldiers and put an end to the discrimination. But by the end of the day, my anger had been replaced by fear as I worried about my village and my family. I closed my eyes and said a prayer, asking God to keep my family safe because I didn't know how I would survive without them.

Many of the students had relatives in the north, where the fighting was worst, so the school director allowed us to listen to radio reports and keep up with events. But more often than not, the national radio broadcasted little more than hate propaganda. The announcers claimed that the rebel soldiers lived in the forest like animals, ate human flesh, and consorted with monkeys. They said that the rebels had become so evil that horns had sprouted from their heads. Rwandans were warned to be on their guard because the "rebel cockroaches" were cunning and could strike anytime, anywhere. These reports inflamed the hyperactive imaginations of already-frightened schoolgirls. One of them was so nervous that she almost got me killed.

Danida, one of my dorm sisters, believed every horrible depiction of the rebel soldiers. One night I must have woken her as I slipped out of bed to use the outdoor bathroom. It was cold, so I had a large scarf wrapped around my head and was wearing oversized pajamas to keep warm. I must have looked a little frightening because when I tried to open the dorm door to get back inside, Danida slammed it shut in my face. The entire campus soon echoed with her terrified screams.

"Help me! Help me! Oh my God, help! It's an RPF soldier—he's come to kill us, to eat us . . . he has horns on his head!"

I recognized Danida's shrieking voice, and calmly said, "Danida, it's me, Immaculée. I'm not a soldier. I don't have horns—I'm wearing a scarf!"

I heard the sound of heavy footsteps on gravel and spun around. The school's biggest security guard was charging toward me in the dark, holding a spear leveled directly at my heart. My knees buckled, and I dropped to the ground. He stopped just inches from me.

"Jesus Christ, Immaculée, I almost killed you! Who the hell is screaming like that?" he said.

By that time *every* girl in the dorm was screaming, and I had to shout for him to hear me over the din. Several security guards spent at least half an hour trying to convince the girls that it was safe to open the door, but they refused. The school director had to be summoned with a master key; once inside, she gave us a long lecture on the dangers of letting our imaginations get the better of us.

Not all the tension in the school was in our imaginations, though. One afternoon we all went out for a picnic and were passing a group of local Hutus. One of the men was holding a big knife and waved it at me. "Look at how tall this one is," he growled. "We'll kill you first. We'll make you pay for what your rebel brothers are doing!"

My stomach churned, and I thought I was about to throw up. It was the first time anyone had threatened me with violence, and I didn't know how to react. I ran back to my dorm, swearing that I'd never go on a school outing again. I cursed my height and wondered why being tall was such a crime in my country. What was I supposed to do? I couldn't stop being tall, and I couldn't stop being a Tutsi!

Clementine came up to me between classes the next day and whispered in my ear, "Come with me, Immaculée. I want to show you what we should do when people like that man with the knife come looking for us."

She led me to a room in a restricted utility building and opened a high-voltage electrical box. "There's more than 1,500 volts of electricity in here," she explained. "If Hutu extremists invade the school and we have no way to escape, we can come here, pull down this lever, and stick our hands in. We'll die immediately—it's better to be electrocuted than be tortured, raped, and murdered. I don't intend to let savages play with my body before they kill me. Don't look so surprised—I've heard too many stories of Tutsi women being raped and abused during bad times not to have an escape plan."

I nodded in agreement. It was strange to talk about ending our lives when we were just 19 years old, but it seemed better than the alternative. Clementine and I made a pact and swore that we'd tell no one else in case the school authorities got wind of our scheme and locked up the electrical box.

WE CONTINUED TO LISTEN TO THE RADIO FOR NEWS, but the government station was notorious for its misinformation. We heard that the RPF had fought all the way to Kigali and attacked the presidential palace. The president went on national radio and warned people to stay in their houses until the army had killed all the "cockroach" invaders. Later we learned from the BBC that there hadn't been any RPF soldiers within miles of the capital—President Habyarimana had invented the attack and lied on the radio in order to have an excuse for arresting thousands of Tutsis, simply because they had relatives living outside the country. The president seemed paranoid, convinced that any Tutsi with a cousin in Uganda must be collaborating with the rebels.

The BBC reported that so many innocent Tutsis had been arrested that all the jails in Rwanda were overflowing and there was no room left for the criminals. It was said that many of the Tutsi prisoners were being starved and tortured, and that some of them had been killed.

When I went home at Christmas, I learned that my own father had been one of those arrested. As I stepped off the bus in Mataba, I bumped into Madame Sirake, one of our longtime neighbors and a legendary gossip. "Come and hug me, my child!" she cried. "It is so good to see you! You're skin and bones, though—aren't those nuns feeding you?"

"Oh, they feed us well. But I'm looking forward to a good family dinner."

"And I'm sure your father will be especially happy to see you after all that's happened to him."

"What do you mean?"

"Haven't you heard, child?"

My heart raced. I hadn't seen my parents since the war began and hadn't had much news from home in weeks.

"I thought surely you would know," Madame Sirake said. "Your dad was in prison."

I sat down heavily on a tree trunk. I couldn't imagine what my father could have done to end up in jail . . . other than being Tutsi. I worried about my mother's health, as the stress of Dad being arrested could easily have triggered another serious asthma attack. I made the 30-minute walk home in record time and found my mother waiting for me at the door.

"How are you, sweetheart?" she asked as she enveloped me in a huge hug. She made no mention of my father's arrest—she always shielded us from unpleasantness, and I could see that she would never change.

"You must be hungry, Immaculée. Why don't you take a shower and I'll make you something to eat? Damascene and Vianney are out together somewhere, and Aimable isn't back from university yet. Your father's at work, but I know he's anxious to see you."

"Is everyone okay? Has anything happened to anyone?"

"Everyone is just fine."

"For heaven's sake, Mom! I already know that Dad was in prison, so stop pretending and tell me what happened."

My mother was so relieved she didn't have to break the bad news to me that she sat right down and told me the whole story.

Shortly after the war began, four government soldiers pushed their way into my father's workplace, tied his arms behind his back, and hauled him off to the Kibuye town jail, locking him up along with half a dozen of his Tutsi friends. The guards were ordered not to feed them or give them water for several days. Eventually, Dad managed to bribe the Hutu guard to take a message to my aunt Cecile, who lived nearby. Cecile brought food to the jail and paid the guard to slip it to my father and his friends.

Two weeks later, my father found out that his arrest was ordered by his old friend Kabayi, a Hutu who had become the district burgo-master (a kind of regional "super mayor," and a very powerful politician). Kabayi and my dad had attended school together and were best friends as children. It was only after President Habyarimana bowed to international pressure and agreed to release thousands of wrongly imprisoned Tutsi prisoners that Kabayi went to the jail and ordered the guards to free Dad and his friends. Kabayi had told the guards not to feed my dad, so he was shocked to see that he was still alive. But he pretended to be upset and apologized profusely, claiming that it had been a terrible misunderstanding.

Later that night, while we were sitting around after dinner, I tried to discuss what had happened with my father, and he said, "It was a mix-up. Kabayi was just acting on orders; it wasn't anything personal. These things are very political, and it's best you kids don't get mixed up in them. Let's forget about the whole thing."

My brothers couldn't believe that our father was so forgiving. They'd known Kabayi their entire lives and were outraged that he'd turned on our dad.

"Kabayi was your friend, Dad. Imagine what might have happened if he were your enemy! Why are you sticking up for him? These people you're defending want to kill you! We should leave the country until the war is over. At the very least, we should get Mom and Immaculée away from here—I'm worried about them," Aimable said.

"No, no, you're overreacting—everyone is safe. Things are better than they used to be, and this is just politics. Don't you kids worry. Everything will be fine, you'll see," Dad assured us.

My mother pleaded with my brothers not to sneak off and join the RPF rebels as so many other young Tutsi men were doing: "If any of you boys go off to fight with the rebels, I want you to know it would kill me, *it would kill me!* If you don't mind killing your mother, then go right ahead, join the rebels. But if you love me, you'll each promise me right now that you won't disappear and leave me in agony. Now do it—promise me!"

Mom had worked herself into such a state that my brothers promised her over and over that they wouldn't join the rebels.

I went back to Lycée, finished my last few months of high school, and wrote the university entrance exam. Once again, I had excellent marks and aced the test, but I held little hope of getting in. The ethnic balance was one of the things RPF was fighting to end, but at the moment it looked as though it would put an end to my academic career.

I said good-bye to my wonderful friends at Lycée and headed home for the summer to wait and see where fate would lead me. The war was intensifying; the rebels were winning more battles and pressuring the government to allow exiled Rwandans to return to the country and share power with the Hutus.

My mother was becoming so traumatized by what was happening that she began consulting psychics. I remember one coming to the house and sitting with Mom in the kitchen. My mother asked her if the war would end and if we'd have peace again.

"I see thunderstorms around us now, but these are just baby storms," the psychic told her. "The mother storm is coming. When she arrives, her lightning will scorch the land, her thunder will deafen us, and her heavy rain will drown us all. The storm will last for three months and many will die. Those who escape will find no one to turn to—every friendly face will have perished."

CHAPTER 4

Off to University

Late in the summer of 1991, the impossible happened: I was awarded a scholarship to the National University in Butare. I had dreamed of going to university my entire life, and suddenly it was a reality, despite all the obstacles placed in front of me.

When my parents heard the news, they were so excited that they couldn't sit still. They rushed around preparing food and drinks so that we could celebrate in proper Rwandan style—with a feast!

"You are the first girl in the family to go to university, so we have to let everyone know about this right away!" Dad shouted, bursting with pride. He arranged for me to go on a long road trip the next day so that I could share the news with my grandmother, aunts and uncles, and all the cousins living in the surrounding villages.

We stayed up all evening laughing, eating, and talking about all the good things that lay ahead. My parents seemed very young to me that night, as though a weight had been lifted from their shoulders.

My mother was beaming. "Everything is looking bright for you, Immaculée," she said. "You will always be able to make your own way now, hold your head high, and never be forced to rely on someone else to put food on your table."

Dad toasted me and offered plenty of fatherly advice: "It's mostly men studying at university, and they won't expect you to be as smart as they are. But I know that you can do as well as, or better than, any man. Because you are Tutsi, getting to university has been a battle, but the hard part is over. Now it's up to you—study hard and pray; and be the disciplined, kind, beautiful daughter we've had the pleasure of watching grow up."

My heart swelled at his sweet, tender words. "Don't worry, Dad," I said. "I won't let you or Mom down. I'll make you proud."

I wanted to study psychology and philosophy so that I could learn about the inner workings of the human heart and mind, but the scholarships were limited to open spaces in specific programs, and I wasn't allowed to choose my own major. The government assigned me to the applied science program, which was fine. I'd pushed myself at Lycée to excel in math and physics to show up my brothers, and now it would pay off. I packed my bags and was soon off to Butare, four hours southeast of my village, and a whole new life away.

WHEN I ARRIVED ON CAMPUS, I discovered that six of my girlfriends from Lycée, including Clementine, had also been awarded scholarships. My friend Sarah had already been studying there for a year and had been waiting for me so that we could be roommates. After all those years of sleeping in crowded dorms, it was a treat to share a room with only one other girl. Clementine visited our room often, and we'd joke about how lucky we were not to have carried out our plan to electrocute ourselves during the early days of the war; otherwise, we'd have missed all the excitement of university.

I loved my classes and studied hard, but I also enjoyed the fun and freedom of being at university. My scholarship included a monthly allowance, which was the equivalent of 30 American dollars—a fortune to me. For the first time in my life I felt independent, like a grown-up. I didn't have to wear a school uniform anymore and could afford to go to town and shop for pretty clothes with my friends. It was exhilarating!

My social life was very active, including gatherings at coffee shops, movies on the weekends, and campus dances every other Saturday night. I joined the drama club, singing and dancing in all the productions, which were often attended by the mayor of Butare. My favorite roles were the religious ones, and once I even got to portray my favorite saint, the Virgin Mary. And I always made time to pray. More and more I found that devotion and meditation balanced me and helped me focus. I attended church several times a week and formed a prayer group with my girlfriends.

I was too busy to be homesick, but lonely letters from my father made me realize that I had to visit more often. Vianney was now away at boarding school, and my parents were having a hard time adjusting. "It's just not the same without any of my children around," Dad wrote. "The house is so empty. Sometimes your mother and I look at each other and wonder, 'Where did all the laughter go?' When you have children of your own, Immaculée, make sure that you enjoy every minute because they're gone too soon. . . ."

I also met a fellow student named John, who knew some of my friends in Mataba. He was three years older than I was, and had a strange habit of "accidentally" bumping into me every day. He started carrying my books, showing me around campus, and introducing me to his friends. He was a nice-looking young man, and very polite and thoughtful. We went for long walks through the forest together and talked about what was important to us: God, family, and a good education. We started dating, and over the next couple of years became quite serious about each other. John was Hutu, but it was never an issue. My father was more concerned that John was a Protestant and the son of a minister.

"Don't forget that you're Catholic," Dad reminded me. "John sounds like a good boy, and you have my blessing to date him—as long as he doesn't try to convert you." Dad was a very tolerant man, but he was also a dyed-in-the-wool Catholic.

My first two years at university flew by, and all was well. My grades were good, my family was healthy, and my life was fun and exciting. In fact, life was so good that it was sometimes easy to forget that there was a war going on—while other times it was impossible to forget.

Despite on-again, off-again peace talks and cease-fires, the fierce fighting between the Tutsi rebels and government troops continued in the north. Radical political parties were springing up in many towns and cities, each violently opposed to the others. Unemployed young men flocked to the youth wings of the different parties because they had nothing better to do. Many were just street-gang members who joined the parties for free drugs and alcohol.

President Habyarimana's own political party organized a youth movement called the *Interahamwe,* which means "those who attack together." The Interahamwe attracted thousands of homeless kids, and its membership spread across the country like a virus. It became the Hutu-extremist militia, and many of its members were trained to fight

33

and kill by government-army soldiers. They traveled in packs and wore informal uniforms—baggy print shirts of bright red, yellow, and green that resembled the flag of their political party. But no matter how much they organized, I always viewed them as lawless street thugs.

I first noticed the Interahamwe during my Easter vacation in 1993. I was in Kigali with John, visiting Sarah and her parents, when the bus we were traveling in became stuck in traffic. As we waited, I glanced out the window and saw a group of young men surrounding a middle-aged Tutsi woman who looked as if she was heading home from shopping. The boys casually took the poor lady's purse, pulled off her jewelry, stole her packages, and knocked her down. Then they yanked off her shoes and ripped off her dress. It was a busy street in the middle of the day, but no one dared to help her. Everyone just looked the other way.

I jumped up from my seat and started shouting out the window for them to stop, but John pulled me down. "Don't say anything!" he ordered. "You have no idea what's going on in this city, Immaculée. You don't want to get mixed up with those guys—they will kill you."

"John, we should do *something*. At least get the police."

"The police won't do anything. These Interahamwe are part of the government. Don't talk to them, don't even look at them—especially since you're Tutsi."

I felt disgusted and helpless. The boys walked away, and I watched as the poor woman struggled to get up off the ground. She limped away in her bare feet, wearing only her tights and a shawl.

If we let devils like these control our streets, we're in deep trouble, I thought as I watched the woman disappear up the road.

A few months later, I had an even more disturbing encounter. Damascene and I had traveled from Mataba to Kigali for a wedding. It was a long, hot, dusty bus trip, and we'd almost reached our destination when the bus came to a sudden stop.

At least 300 Interahamwe were standing in the road blocking our way, all of them looking ridiculous in their clownish outfits, but dangerously wild-eyed as well. Many of them seemed to be drunk or on drugs, as they danced around in circles, yelling and cursing at passersby. Our driver was too frightened to go forward, so he announced that he was turning the bus around. He said that we could stay aboard with him and take a two-hour detour, or get out and walk.

"Let's just stay on the bus," Damascene said. "Those people look insane." But I didn't want to stay for many reasons, mainly because I refused to be intimidated by a bunch of hooligans.

"We have to get off or we'll miss the wedding," I told him. "We can walk to the church in no time."

We disembarked, along with half of the other passengers. Once outside, we saw that many of the Interahamwe were holding machetes while checking the identity cards of people who wanted to walk past them. I felt a surge of anger and asked, "What gives them the right?"

Damascene was worried. "I think we should go back, Immaculée. I've heard bad things about these guys. Let's walk home."

"*Walk home?* It took us four hours by bus to get here, and it would take us three days to walk home. Besides, these people can't just set themselves up as police and bully us because we're Tutsi."

I was less worried about the Interahamwe than I was about the frightened look on Damascene's face. He almost always had a jovial expression, and was probably the bravest person I knew. But I saw then that he was really scared. Normally *I* would have been asking *him* what to do, but something pushed me to go forward.

"Let's walk on through," I said. "We'll be fine."

"How do you know that? What makes you think they won't just kill us? The government allows them to do what they want. The police don't touch them."

"Let's do what you always suggest when we have a problem, Damascene. Let's pray and trust that God will protect us."

We stood on the side of the road and prayed, 30 feet away from the mob of angry extremists. I asked God to excuse the short notice, but we needed His help to get to the church safely. I walked toward the roadblock, and a couple of the young men noticed me and tapped their machetes against their thighs.

"Oh, no, Immaculée . . . are you sure about this?"

"Yes, yes, just act naturally—and maybe you better get your rosary out of your pocket."

I held my own rosary tightly in my hand as we walked toward the Interahamwe. About a dozen of them surrounded us, looked me up and down, and demanded to see our identity cards. I stared at them straight in the eye, smiled, and handed over the documents. I could see that I confused them by being so bold—they couldn't understand why a Tutsi woman wasn't afraid of them or their machetes. They handed back our cards and let us pass, but I never forgot the fear I saw in Damascene's eyes. It was the first time I'd seen him falter, and I couldn't shake the feeling that something evil had arrived in Rwanda.

A month after our roadblock experience, President Habyarimana traveled to Tanzania and signed a peace agreement with the Tutsi rebels. The agreement would end the civil war and give Tutsis a role in governing the country. It sounded wonderful—I thought that Rwanda might find peace, and that Tutsis and Hutus could finally live in harmony as equals.

But the promise of peace triggered more protests and threats of greater violence to come. The minute the agreement was signed, one of Rwanda's most powerful military officers, a scary-looking colonel named Theoneste Bagosora—who was also the chief leader of the Interahamwe—stormed out of the talks. Bagosora was disgusted by seeing President Habyarimana shake hands with RPF leader Paul Kagame, whom he called a "Tutsi snake." He vowed that he'd never make peace with the Tutsis and promised to return to Rwanda "to prepare an apocalypse."

And that's exactly what he did.

➤◄

CHAPTER 5

Returning Home

Too many mornings I awoke to the sound of hatred. I'd sleep peacefully until the obnoxious sounds of RTLM drifted through my dorm window and into my dreams. You see, in my third year at university, RTLM became the new, ultra-popular radio station among extremist Hutus. It was little more than a radical hate machine, spewing out anti-Tutsi venom.

It was always some disembodied, malevolent voice calling for "Hutu Power"—the catchphrase for Hutus to rise up against their Tutsi friends and neighbors: "These Tutsi cockroaches are out to kill us. Do not trust them . . . we Hutus must act first! They are planning to take over our government and persecute us. If anything happens to our president, then we must exterminate all the Tutsis right away! Every Hutu must join together to rid Rwanda of these Tutsi cockroaches! Hutu Power! Hutu Power!"

It was an awful way to wake up, but the broadcasts were so ridiculously juvenile that they were almost funny. It was hard to believe that anyone could take the infantile insults and outlandish threats seriously; still, it was unsettling to know that the government was allowing Tutsis to be openly threatened over the public airwaves. But at the time, I was more disturbed by rumors that Tutsis were being murdered by extremists in several areas of the country.

Like my friends on campus, I tried not to dwell on the media reports. Easter was approaching, and it was always a special time for my family. We'd spend it together at home, entertaining neighbors and visiting friends and relatives. I'd never missed an Easter get-together before, but I wanted to stay at school to prepare for my upcoming exams. I was determined to do well on them.

Because my parents didn't have a phone, I wrote Dad a letter explaining why I wouldn't be home. My parents had always insisted that their children study extra hard to get ahead, so I was sure they wouldn't mind.

I couldn't have been more wrong.

Dad wrote back, begging me to come home. In fact, he asked me to come *immediately* and not even wait for the school holidays to begin. He wrote that he wanted me to be with him, and he promised that I could study at home with no disturbances. His heartfelt plea brought tears to my eyes:

> *My darling daughter,*
> *I feel like school has taken you away from us. Your mom*
> *and I wait so impatiently for your vacation to begin because it*
> *means we can have you home and live like a family again. We*
> *need your presence; we are your parents, and we love you and*
> *miss you terribly—never forget that! Even if it can be only for*
> *two days, you must come to see us; don't sacrifice the time for*
> *anything else. We need you with us. . . .*

Before I'd finished his letter, I'd decided to go home. I planned to spend six days with my parents and be back at school for my exams at the end of the week. While I made my travel arrangements, Sarah's younger brother, Augustine, asked if he could come home with me and spend the holidays with my family. Augustine was good friends with my brother Vianney, and he'd been staying in our dorm room since the semester ended at his high school in Kigali. He was a tall, handsome, and very sweet 18-year-old boy who was shy around everyone except Vianney. I told him that we'd be delighted to have him as our guest.

AUGUSTINE AND I ARRIVED IN MATABA on Saturday afternoon, and my parents were overjoyed to have me home. The entire family was there with the exception of Aimable, who'd won an international scholarship to do postgraduate work in science. He'd actually left the country to study in Senegal, more than 3,000 miles away. Damascene had traveled down from Kigali, where he'd been teaching high school since graduating with his master's degree in history, and Vianney was home on vacation from boarding school.

I spent the first day back catching up on local gossip with Damascene, visiting friends, and arguing playfully with Vianney. The next day was Easter Sunday, and we had a beautiful meal together. We thanked God for all that He had blessed us with and prayed for the well-being of everyone in our family and our village—and we said a special prayer for Aimable, our only absent member. Despite the political tension in the air, we were having a great time. I felt safe and secure with my parents, knowing that whatever might happen, my mother would be there to comfort us and my dad would be there to protect us. At least, that's what I thought.

It was such a typical evening that it was hard to believe our world was about to change forever. We were sitting in the living room chatting about school, work, and what had been happening in the village. Mom updated us on the crops, and Dad told us about the kids his coffee co-op was sponsoring for scholarships. Augustine and Vianney goofed around, making jokes with each other, and I relaxed and took it all in, happy just to be home.

The only person who wasn't having a good time was Damascene. He was usually the life of the party, but he'd been pensive and anxious all evening.

"Damascene, what's wrong with you tonight?" I asked.

My brother looked up at me, and when our eyes met, he couldn't keep quiet any longer. He unburdened himself to me in a rush of words and emotion: "Immaculée, I saw them, I saw the killers. I was on my way to Bonn's house, and we saw them in the distance. They were wearing the bright colors of the Interahamwe and were carrying hand grenades. They had *grenades,* Immaculée!" His voice was hoarse.

The room had grown silent, since everyone had overheard him. My parents looked at each other, then back at Damascene.

"Maybe you're letting your imagination get the better of you," my father said, trying to calm his son down. "There is a lot of dangerous talk going on, and people are seeing danger where there is none."

"No, I'm not imagining things," Damascene said, getting to his feet and speaking with urgency. "And that's not all I saw. They have a list of names of all the Tutsi families in the area, and our names are on it! It's a death list! They are planning to start killing everyone on the list tonight!"

Damascene paced around the room and began pleading with my father. "Dad, we have to leave, *please.* We have to get out of here while we still can. We can just walk down the hill, find a boat, cross Lake Kivu, and be safely in Zaire by midnight. But we have to leave now before it's too late."

Damascene's outburst was so sudden and out of character that he startled us all. Knowing my brother, he must have been brooding all evening over what he'd seen during the afternoon, but didn't want to say anything to us until he'd come up with an escape plan.

"Hold on, Damascene, just settle down a minute," my father said. "You're upsetting your mother and sister. Let's analyze exactly what it is you think you saw and heard today. If you make decisions when you're panicked or afraid, you'll make mistakes. Let's go over everything carefully. Did you actually see this list?"

Damascene was distressed by my father's doubts, but admitted that he hadn't seen the list with his own eyes—he'd heard about it from friends. But he was positive the people he'd seen were Interahamwe.

"You see, it's like I thought," my father said. "Everyone is on edge, and your nerves are making things seem worse than they are. I've seen this situation before. You hear rumors of death squads and stories about death lists, but after a few days you realize it has all been greatly exaggerated. I'm not about to pack up my family and run away from rumors. We are not going to abandon our home and everything we've worked for because nervous people have vivid imaginations."

"But, Dad," I piped in, "Damascene isn't the nervous type. He's smart and isn't fooled easily. Maybe we should listen to him."

I was getting worried. If it was true that the Interahamwe had a death list and would start killing people that night, then they could be coming for us at any minute.

"Perhaps we should do as Damascene says," I urged my father. "Think of all the things we've been hearing on the radio. I haven't taken them seriously, but that might have been a mistake. They say that all Tutsis should be killed. Maybe Damascene is right—maybe we should leave now!"

"No, Immaculée, we shouldn't leave. Things are getting better with the government, and there will be peace soon. Those people on the radio are crazy; no one is taking them seriously! Don't worry. Let's just stay calm and enjoy the holidays. There is no death list, and no one is coming to kill us. I'm older and I know better," my father said, with a weak smile. "Now, for heaven's sake, let's sit down and eat dinner together."

My father's assurances temporarily convinced me that all would be fine, and we all gathered around the dining room table to eat. I sensed that Damascene was unmoved by our father's arguments, although he was putting on a brave front and acting like his old self—singing silly songs, making jokes about people in our village, and teasing Vianney about his girlfriends. But the more he made us laugh, the more certain I was that he was playacting. Behind his beautiful, open smile, my brother was deeply troubled.

I wish I had known that that night was to be our last family supper together. I would have stood up and thanked God for all of them. I would have told everyone sitting around that table how much I loved them and thanked them for loving me. But I didn't know.

BEFORE WE WENT TO BED, we said evening prayers together as a family, as we'd always done. My mother kissed us goodnight, and my father promised that nothing bad would happen and wished us a peaceful sleep.

As soon as we heard our parents' bedroom door close, the four of us—Damascene, Vianney, Augustine, and me—assembled in the living room. We talked for at least an hour about the rumors Damascene had heard and the things he'd seen that day. We were worried about my father's reluctance to take Damascene's fears seriously.

"I don't mean any disrespect to your father," Augustine whispered, "and I know that I'm not supposed to argue with my elders, but I think your dad is wrong. I agree with Damascene—I think staying here is dangerous. If your family's name is on the death list, they will come for you, and there's nothing we can do to stop them! I don't think your father is going to change his mind about leaving, so maybe we should leave, right now, without your parents."

Everyone was quiet. I'm sure that we all wanted to run to Lake Kivu and hop into a rowboat, but my brothers and I couldn't leave our parents without saying good-bye. And we were so accustomed to our father making the decisions in the household that it was natural for us to follow his lead. Besides, we reasoned, it was getting so late that Augustine and Vianney were falling asleep in their chairs. So Damascene and I decided that we should wait until morning and talk to Dad again, and then we all headed to bed.

My bedroom was like my own little chapel. With my Bible and statues of Jesus and the Virgin Mary on my night table, it was a place where I connected with God and my own spiritual energies. I knelt by my bed and looked at the statues, saying a prayer to God to protect my family from danger.

Also sitting in front of me was a birthday card that I'd bought for Damascene. His 27th birthday was coming up, and I'd been trying for days to write a poem for him that said how much I loved and admired him. Our parents didn't teach us to openly express our love for one another, but I intended to change that. And who better to start with than Damascene, whom I cherished so dearly and who inspired me more than anyone else in the world?

When we were young, Damascene would scold me if I acted foolishly or spoiled. His words stung and annoyed me, but later, when I'd think over what he said, I'd realize he was right. Even as a child, he had a gift for teaching, and he possessed wisdom beyond his years. As a teenager, I used to pray for God to make me more like him, with his beautiful soul and giving heart. I watched him give his clothes to the poor and spend hours comforting people who were outcast due to sickness, poverty, or madness.

Damascene was a superstar in our village. And as I lay myself down to sleep that night, I thought about how much my brother meant to me. I picked up my pen and added a few lines to the poem on his birthday card. I grinned, imagining how shy and happy he would be when he read the words. With a smile still on my face, I turned out my light and tried to sleep.

My eyes were shut for what only seemed like minutes when the door of my room burst open. I sat up with a start and noticed that it was dawn. I could see Damascene's terrified face in the gray half-light of my bedroom, and I imagined the worst. "What is it, Damascene? Are the killers here?" I whispered. I could barely hear my own frightened voice.

My brother said nothing. I could hear him trying to catch his breath while he stood in the doorway. When he finally spoke, his voice sounded like it was coming to me from the bottom of a deep well: "Get up, Immaculée—for heaven's sake, get up. The president is dead!"

"What? What do you mean the president is dead?" I cried out. I couldn't believe what I was hearing. The president had promised to bring peace and equality back to Rwanda. How could he be dead?

"I mean President Habyarimana is *dead!* He was killed last night. His plane was shot out of the sky."

I thought of what I'd heard on the radio a few days before: "If anything happens to our president, then all Tutsis must be exterminated!"

I jumped out of bed and searched frantically for something to wear. I pulled on a pair of jeans under my long green nightdress and was so flustered that I actually dressed in front of my brother, something I had never done in my life.

"The president has been killed; someone's killed the president," I kept mumbling to myself in dazed disbelief. I pushed the curtains away from my bedroom window and looked outside. I'm not sure if it was my imagination, but I saw a sickly yellow haze settling over the village.

"Even the sky is changing," I said, dropping onto the bed and holding my head in my hands. "Oh, Damascene, we are all going to die. They will come for us now and will kill us for sure."

My brother sat down and put his arms around me. "Listen to me, Immaculée, we are *not* going to die," he firmly stated. "We had nothing to do with this. The president was flying back from peace talks in Tanzania, and he was traveling with the president of Burundi. The plane was shot down when it was landing in Kigali . . . *in Kigali!* No one will be blaming us down here."

Damascene was trying to be brave for me, but he was a poor actor. I know that he was trying to convince himself as much as me.

"Maybe things will improve for us now that he's dead," he continued. "So many people were against these peace negotiations and President Habyarimana's plans for a more moderate government that his death may actually ease the tensions. Don't be so frightened, Immaculée. Come outside. Everyone is out there listening to the radio."

43

He took me by the hand, and we went out into the yard where my parents, Vianney, and Augustine had settled in to listen to the radio. The announcer reported that roadblocks and military checkpoints had been set up all over the capital, minutes after the president's plane had been blown up. He also said that at least 20 Tutsi families in Kigali had been killed during the night.

I hesitate to use the word *reported* because the man on the radio sounded more like a cheerleader for the killers than a journalist. When he announced that presidential guard soldiers had taken it upon themselves to kill Tutsis to avenge the president's death, he made the killings sound justified. He made it sound like dragging entire families into the street and murdering them was perfectly reasonable.

Then he read out some of the names of the people that the soldiers had killed so far in Kigali. The fifth name belonged to my Uncle Twaza.

"They've killed Twaza?" my mother cried out, quickly covering her eyes with her hands and shaking her head in disbelief. "Why would they kill Twaza? He's never harmed anyone."

A painful silence enveloped my family as we realized that we'd missed our opportunity to escape the night before. My father tried again to ease our fears. "Emotions are running very high in the capital. That's where the killings are because that's where most of the soldiers are based," he said, matter-of-factly. "Everything will settle down in a day or two, you'll see."

"I think I would like to go home now," said Augustine, whose family lived in Kigali. We looked at him, knowing that it was far too dangerous to go anywhere. A few minutes later our suspicions were confirmed in a series of radio announcements: "Stay in your homes. It is forbidden to travel. Only military personnel will be allowed in the streets. Do not go outside. Public transportation has been suspended. *Do not leave your homes!*"

"They want us to stay put so they'll know where to find us. They want us to be sitting ducks!" Damascene exclaimed, eyes widening. "If our names are on their death list, then they'll know where we live, and they know we will be here."

It was the morning of April 7, 1994. We didn't know it yet, but the genocide had begun.

>«

CHAPTER 6

No Going Back

Mom, Dad, Damascene, Vianney, Augustine, and I spent the entire day huddled together in our yard listening to the radio. The broadcasts from outside of Rwanda reported that ordinary Hutu citizens were joining government soldiers and Interahamwe militiamen and killing innocent Tutsi civilians; meanwhile, the local stations were encouraging Hutus to pick up machetes and attack their Tutsi neighbors.

I felt like a lost little girl waiting for my parents to give me instructions. I thought that since they'd survived the many political upheavals and Tutsi massacres since 1959, they must know what to do.

The national radio station continued to warn people to remain in their homes, and like good children, we obeyed. We were too afraid to open our gate to find out was happening on the other side of the fence. We placed ourselves under self-imposed house arrest, worried that stepping beyond our property line could prove fatal.

My family didn't own a telephone, and even if we had, most of the phone lines in the country were down. We were completely cut off, except for whatever the radio told us. We sat listening to the horrific reports for hours, until I thought I'd go out of my mind. Late in the afternoon, I pulled out my books and began studying for my exams.

"How do you do it, Immaculée?" Damascene asked. "Where do you find the strength to study? Why do you believe that there will even be a school to go back to?"

My brother had helped me shake my own despair only hours earlier, but now he too was hopeless. It was my turn to be strong. "Stop worrying," I said. "We'll get through this. If things get bad, we'll slip across the border. Mom and Dad have been through this before. Have faith."

The truth was that I had little faith myself—I wasn't studying to prepare for exams, but to keep my mind off my family's worries.

The only encouraging news we heard all day was a message from the RPF's Paul Kagame, who was in charge of the Tutsi rebel soldiers based in Uganda. He promised that if the killing of Tutsis didn't stop, the rebels would invade Rwanda and fight to the death to protect their fellow Tutsis. It was comforting to hear Kagame say that, but I was saddened that the only "good" news was the threat of all-out war.

None of us slept more than a few minutes that night.

The next day we listened to a BBC phone interview with Rwanda's prime minister, Agathe Uwilingiyimana, a moderate Hutu living in Kigali. Even though United Nations peacekeepers were guarding her, there was gunfire all around her home. She said that she, her husband, and their five children were lying on the floor and had no way to escape. During the interview, the phone line went dead. We learned later that soldiers had burst into her home and shot both her and her husband. Luckily, her children had been rescued.

The prime minister's words affected us deeply, and it was now impossible to pretend that things were going to get better. If killers could execute the Hutu prime minister, what would stop them from murdering us?

The constant tension during those 24 hours took a toll on my family. My mother went into a kind of trance and began moving from room to room, packing every suitcase we owned with whatever she could lay her hands on. "I'm not going to leave the things I've worked so hard for so that people can steal them," she told us. "I'm going to hide them away. One day we'll come back for them."

I didn't know where she was planning to go—we'd just heard over the radio that our only practical escape route (across Lake Kivu) had been cut off by the Interahamwe militia. They were murdering every Tutsi or moderate Hutu who approached the lake.

My father remained in bewildered denial. "If the killing continues," he reasoned, "the RPF will step in to stop it. They could be here in Mataba to protect us in a few days."

"Daddy, what are you thinking?" I asked him, incredulous. "The RPF soldiers are up north near the Ugandan border. They have no vehicles; they're on foot and will have to fight the army and Interahamwe every step of the way. It will take weeks for them to get here . . . *if* they get here at all!"

I could count the number of times I'd contradicted my father on one hand, but everything was changing. My parents weren't thinking clearly, and Augustine and Vianney were too young and scared to depend upon. I'd followed Damascene's lead my entire life, but now he'd retreated to his room and was staring at the walls.

"Do you honestly think we're going to escape this?" he asked when I came to find him. "I'm lying here trying to picture what I'll be doing next year, but I can't. I don't think I'll be alive. I have no future."

"Damascene, you have to snap out of this!" I shouted. "You can't give up before we even start to fight! If you can't see what you'll be doing next year, I can! You'll be with me in Butare when I graduate university. You're going to be sitting in the front row clapping and cheering when I accept my diploma. So please, get up and help Mom and Dad!"

"I wish I had your faith and courage," he muttered, then continued staring at the wall.

I didn't feel courageous, but someone had to pull my family together. I tried to be strong and at least *act* brave so that the family wouldn't collapse in complete despair.

By nightfall we'd heard that the ten Belgian UN peacekeepers protecting the prime minister had been murdered by government soldiers and that the lives of all the other Belgians in Rwanda were being threatened. We knew that if the Belgians and other foreigners left the country, there would be no one capable of stopping an all-out slaughter. For the second night in a row, none of us slept.

AT DAWN, THE SCREAMING BEGAN. Two-dozen Interahamwe militiamen attacked our village, tossing grenades into houses. When the families inside tried to escape, they were hacked to death with machetes.

When my family heard the screams, we opened our gate and ran out to the road. We could see for quite a distance from our hilltop home and searched for the source of the commotion. Below us, on the far side of a nearby river, we saw a group of Interahamwe surrounding one of our neighbors. They moved like a pack of jackals, holding their machetes above their heads and circling him slowly. We watched helplessly from afar as they moved in for the kill, mercilessly chopping him to bits.

We turned away from the murder in horror. Coming toward us quickly from the other side of the hill were dozens of our Tutsi neighbors. The men were carrying sticks and stones to protect their families, while the women carried their babies in their arms and yelled at their older kids not to fall behind.

"Leonard! Leonard!" they called when they saw my father. "Please help us. They're killing us! What will we do? Where should we go?"

Since my father was one of the most respected men in the village, within a few hours approximately 2,000 men, women, and children were camped out in front of our house, looking to him for guidance. I couldn't believe how many people had been driven from their homes. Scores of families sat around cooking fires, arguing about what to do next, while their children played games and chased each other through the fields. If it hadn't been for the occasional gunfire and grenades exploding in the distance, the gathering could easily have been mistaken for a family picnic.

The number of people who had come seeking my father's help and advice seemed to bring him back to reality. He became more like himself and took action. "Everyone be calm," he said. "We'll find a way to get through this together."

THAT NIGHT MY FATHER TOLD ME HE WAS concerned for my health. "You haven't slept at all, Immaculée. The rest of us are going to stay outside tonight with the others, so I want you go to your room and get some sleep."

"But Dad, I . . ." I didn't like the idea of staying in the house alone. I was terrified that we'd be attacked in the night.

He saw my hesitation and smiled. "Don't worry, my sweetheart. I'm here, and I'm going to protect you. It's cold outside, and you need to get some rest. Now go inside and lie down."

I knew that he couldn't protect me against the Interahamwe, but I couldn't bear to hurt his pride, so I did as he asked. My mother promised that she'd stand guard over the house to make sure I was safe.

Despite my parents' love and concern, I couldn't sleep at all that night either. I kept a small radio on my chest, spinning the dial until dawn and listening to report after report of what was happening around us. The news got worse as the night wore on: Tutsis were being killed in large numbers in every corner of Rwanda, peace talks between the government and Tutsi rebels had broken off, and the RPF vowed to fight its way to the capital to stop the slaughter.

In the middle of the night I went outside and found my mother asleep in the courtyard. She'd dozed off guarding our front door. When I moved closer to wake her, my breath caught in my throat. She was wrapped in a white bedsheet, and in the cold moonlight she looked like a corpse. I was overwhelmed by the sight and ran back to my room. I fell onto my bed, and for the first time since our nightmare began, I burst into tears.

"Why is this happening?" I cried into my pillow. "What have we done to deserve this? Why is being a Tutsi so wrong? Why are you letting this happen to us, God?"

I felt selfish for crying and dried my eyes. *Silly girl,* I thought, *cry later. This tragedy is just beginning, and there will be plenty of time for tears.*

I returned outside just as the sun was beginning to rise over Lake Kivu and stood beside my sleeping mother. I softly stroked her feet and carefully unknotted the tangles in her hair. Mother was always so beautiful and proud of her appearance—she'd be mortified to be seen in such a state. I kissed her cheek and gently shook her awake. "Mom, get up," I said softly. "It's cold out here. Get into bed."

As soon as she opened her eyes, they filled with fear and confusion. "Where is Damascene? Where is Vianney? Immaculée . . . you should be in the house getting rest. What are you doing outside alone in the dark?" she asked, struggling to get up.

"What are *you* doing out here, Mom?"

"I didn't want to leave you alone in the house, but I didn't want to be too far away from your father or my boys. I have to make sure everyone is safe."

"Everyone *is* safe, Mom. The boys and Dad are camping out with the others. Maybe things will get better today," I said, my heart aching from the pain etched on her face. She'd worked and sacrificed for us her entire life and spent countless hours worrying about our safety. Now she knew she couldn't do anything to protect us, and it was killing her. She seemed to have aged years during the past few days.

We went looking for my father and brothers, who were with the refugees, and we weren't prepared for what we found when we stepped outside. At least 10,000 Tutsis were camped in front of our home.

My father was walking through the huge crowd, greeting people with words of encouragement. He'd been up all night and refused to go inside and rest. He washed, put on fresh clothes, and was right back among the refugees. Dozens of people were trying to reach him, calling out his name, but there were so many that it was impossible for him to talk to them all.

Finally, he climbed to the top of a large boulder at the base of a cliff and turned to the frightened crowd. "Friends, friends!" he shouted. His voice boomed above the multitude.

"I know you're afraid; don't be. These people—these killers—are few, and we are many. They're not stronger than we are, not if we have God's love in our hearts. If they are acting out of evil, if they have come to harm us for no reason other than their hatred for us, then we will defeat them. Love will always conquer hatred. Believe in yourselves, believe in each other, and believe in God!"

My heart swelled with pride. It was hard to believe that this was the same man who had seemed so confused and unreasonable just hours before. Yet here he was, passing his strength on to so many lost and terrified souls.

"We will fight them," Dad continued. The crowd, moved by his words, began chanting his name and cheering him on, but he held up his hand for quiet.

"As I said, if these killers are driven only by hatred, we will force them away. But if the government is sending them, if these attacks are part of an organized plan to exterminate Tutsis, we are in serious trouble. The government has guns and grenades—it has an army and a militia—and we have no weapons at all. If the government plans to kill us, all we can do is pray. Let us use the time we have to repent. Let us pray for God to forgive our sins. If we *are* to die, let us die with our hearts clean."

The cheering stopped and the crowd was silent. At first I thought that my father had crushed their spirits, but I realized that thousands of them had taken his advice and were quietly praying.

"It doesn't matter if we live or die—the important thing is that we fight against this evil that has come to our homes!" my dad cried out.

As thousands of eyes were glued to him, he lifted his right hand high above his head. I could see that he was holding his red and white rosary.

"We will ask God to defend us against evil," he shouted, waving the rosary in the air. Then he reached down and picked up a long, metal-tipped spear with his left hand. He lifted the spear about his head as well and continued, "We will ask God for help, but we will also defend ourselves. Find a spear, arm yourselves, but don't kill anyone! We won't be like them—we will not kill—but we won't sit around and be slaughtered like sheep either. Let us be strong . . . and let us pray."

A FEW HOURS AFTER MY FATHER'S SPEECH, 50 Interahamwe armed with knives and machetes attacked the Tutsis outside our home. My father gathered more than 100 Tutsi men together and rushed toward the killers. When they got within throwing distance, they tossed stones at them and eventually chased them away. But it was a minor victory—the radio continued to report widespread killings, and a steady stream of Tutsi refugees was arriving at our door. Each new arrival had a new horror story; from what they told us, we realized that we were completely surrounded by Interahamwe.

After the attack, I went to my bedroom to get my scapular, a kind of cloth necklace that Catholics wear. The scapular is very precious to me because it's blessed with the Virgin Mary's promise that "whosoever dies wearing it shall not suffer eternal fire. It shall be a sign of salvation, a protection in danger, and a pledge of peace." I bought it when I moved away to university, believing that if anything happened to me, my scapular would speed my journey to heaven.

I went to my father's study, where he'd gone after chasing off the Interahamwe. He was rummaging through his desk and sticking family photos into his pockets.

"Dad, I have something for you," I said, holding out the scapular.

He knew what it was and what it was for. "Why don't we leave it in the house? That way no one will burn it down," he said.

My eyes filled with tears. "No, Dad, *you* have to wear this. Who is the person in this family putting himself in danger? Who is the most likely to be killed in all of this, Dad? Stop worrying about the house—it's your spirit that matters now, not material things."

"All right, Immaculée. I understand," he said, taking the scapular from my hand and putting it around his neck. "Now, what do I have for you? What can I give my only daughter?" he wondered aloud, rifling through his desk. "Ah, of course! I know exactly what to give you."

He reached into his shirt pocket and pulled out the red and white rosary he'd shown to the crowd. He pressed the beads into my palm and covered my hand with his. "Keep it always, Immaculée."

"I will, I promise."

As soon as we exchanged gifts, our front door banged open, and a neighborhood woman began yelling desperately for my father. "Leonard! Leonard! Please come quickly! They're back! The killers are back! But there are many, many more of them now!"

My father ran to his bedroom, grabbed a spear that he had hidden under his bed, and charged out the door. I followed him as best I could, but my legs felt like rubber. I thought that we were about to die . . . especially when I saw that the killers were standing about a quarter mile from our house.

"Let's fight these wicked people! Let's stop this senseless killing! They might kill us, but we'll die pure of heart!" my father cried out, trying to rally other Tutsi men to his side. No one joined him.

Dad was sweating, and his eyes were wide and wild. He began running toward the killers by himself, holding his spear high in the air. My mother flew after him, her long blue dress flapping behind her. She grabbed hold of his shirttail and dug her heels into the earth. He kept running, dragging her behind him as she screamed out his name: "Stop, Leonard! Stop! You can't fight them alone. Please,

please, *please* let someone else go. There are so many young men here. Let *them* fight," she begged.

Everyone was staring at her, but she didn't care. She saw her husband of 28 years—a man she loved above all others—running toward certain death, and she was going to do everything in her power to stop him.

Dad ran out of breath and was unable to drag Mom behind him any farther. He stopped and tried to catch his breath while his wife clung to his shirt. "What is wrong with you?" she shrieked at the younger Tutsis in the crowd. "How can you let your elders fight your battles for you? How can you let my husband get killed for you? Be men—get up and fight!"

People stared at her but made no move to help because they were all terrified. My mother turned to my father, wrapped her arms around him, and pleaded, "Don't go, Leonard, please!"

"Listen to me, Rose." Dad gripped her by the shoulders. "It is my duty to be here for these people right now. If that means fighting, then I will fight. I have to do what I feel is right. Now stop panicking and go help the young mothers with their children. I'll be back."

By the time my parents finished arguing, the killers had left. I suppose that as they got closer, they got a better sense of just how many Tutsis were actually at our house. Even with guns and grenades, 100 against 10,000 were not good odds. But the odds would not be in our favor for long.

AFTER MY PARENTS' SKIRMISH IN FRONT OF THE HOUSE, Damascene came to see me. His eyes were bloodshot and his voice was strained. "The killers ran away this time, Immaculée, but they'll come back. And when they do, there will be too many of them to chase away with sticks and stones. If they catch you, they will rape you first, then kill you. You have to leave. Go stay with Pastor Murinzi . . . I'm sure he'll hide you until this is over."

"No, Damascene. I won't go if it means leaving the family behind. I'll only go if we all go together. I wouldn't be able to live with myself knowing that you could be killed while I was hiding somewhere."

Damascene looked at me with tears in his eyes. He went and got our father and they came to talk to me together. "Your brother is right, Immaculée," Dad said. "You're a young woman, and it's too dangerous for you here. Go to Pastor Murinzi's house, and in a few days when the troubles are over, I will come and get you myself."

I didn't believe that he'd come and get me because, in my heart, I didn't believe that he was going to survive. So I replied, "But I'd rather stay here with you."

"No. You're going into hiding, and that's final." My father ended any further argument.

"What about Mom? She should come with me."

"I've already asked her, but she won't leave your brothers. You'd better take Augustine with you, too—I don't know what I'd say to his parents if anything happened to him while he was staying with us."

Within the hour, Augustine and I were on our way to Pastor Murinzi's house. All I had with me were the clothes on my back, the rosary my father had given to me, and my government-issued identity card that said I was Tutsi.

My father followed behind us for a short distance. As he turned to go back, he shouted, "Remember, Immaculée, I will come get you myself!"

It was the last thing he ever said to me.

It was a five-mile hike down a narrow dirt road to the pastor's house, and we walked quickly. Augustine was a Hutu, but he looked like a Tutsi, and we were worried that we'd run into the killers along the way. About a mile from the pastor's house, we did. There was a mob of at least 100 Hutus coming toward us, carrying spears, knives, and machetes.

"I wish I was a bird and could fly away home to Kigali right now," Augustine whispered as they got closer. My heart pounded against my chest.

Some of the men were banging their machetes together, making a sickening clang. Others dragged their blades along the road, and orange sparks spit up whenever the steel hit a stone. I kept my eyes fixed on the road, but I could see the shadows cast by their weapons.

I wondered if someone was going to stick a spear into my back, and what kind of hole it would make in my flesh. I closed my eyes and waited for the pain . . . but God was watching over us.

"Immaculée, what are you doing out here?"

I opened my eyes and saw Kageyo, a Hutu, but also a good friend of my father's. He was carrying a very big spear, but there was kindness in his eyes.

The Hutus were all around us, and Kageyo yelled at them, "Don't harm these children! They're friends of mine, so no one dare touch them."

The Hutus looked very angry but passed us by.

"Don't worry, children, we will bring the peace back," Kageyo said, and left with the others.

Augustine and I ran as fast as our feet would carry us, and we didn't stop until we were standing in front of the pastor's house.

"We're safe now," I said.

How I wish I had been right.

>*<

CHAPTER 7

The Pastor's House

Augustine and I were fighting for breath when we arrived at Pastor Murinzi's house. I was exhausted from the last few anguished days, and my head was swimming after running at full speed from the killers. When I saw the pastor staring at us from his doorway, I could barely speak. "There were men . . . with spears . . . they were going to . . . " I gasped.

Pastor Murinzi stood on his porch, framed by the enormous front door of his big brick home. I'd always thought that his European-style house seemed out of place in a village that had so many huts and tin shacks—it had many bedrooms, a big living and dining room, and bathrooms with real indoor plumbing. And the front yard overflowed with flowers, which were protected from the summer sun by a huge shade tree.

The pastor greeted us warmly. I shook his hand, still struggling to catch my breath.

"It's good to see you again, Immaculée," he said with a smile. "It's been too long."

I'd been good friends with the youngest of the pastor's ten children since childhood and had visited his house many times. He'd had many business dealings with my father over the years, so I'd seen him at our home as well. Plus, he was also an uncle of my boyfriend, John, so he was far from being a stranger. I suddenly remembered my aunt once telling me that the pastor, who was a Protestant, resented the good works my father did, along with Dad's prominent standing in the community. But he was always polite to me, and I'd always been courteous and respectful to him, so I decided to focus on that.

"My father told me to come here, Pastor Murinzi," I finally said, still gripping his hand. "He said that he'll come for me as soon as things get better. He promised that he'd come for me himself."

The pastor said nothing, but his eyes spoke volumes: *Your father will never come back for you. You'll never see him again.*

I pushed the pastor's look from my mind because if I started thinking about harm coming to my family, I'd break down completely. I introduced him to Augustine before he ushered us into his living room, where several guests were talking to each other. It may have been my imagination, but I thought that the conversation paused when we walked into the room.

The first person I saw was Buhoro, my teacher from primary school. Although he'd humiliated me during ethnic roll call, I hadn't held a grudge. I was so happy and relieved to see someone I knew that I went straight over to him. I gave him a big smile and put my hand out for him to shake.

He looked down at my hand and then up into my eyes before clicking his tongue in disgust and turning his back on me. I was devastated. I'd never been treated so rudely or with such hostile disrespect, and this from a teacher I'd known since grade school! Everyone in the room witnessed what happened. His body language was unmistakable, screaming, *Don't touch me, you piece of Tutsi dirt!*

I looked around, expecting one of the other adults to come to my defense and chastise Buhoro for his behavior. But no one paid any attention—not even the pastor, who was standing right in front of us. Augustine was the only one to act: He walked up to Buhoro and refused to shake hands with *him;* instead, he came and stood by my side.

I'd known for a long time that Buhoro was a Hutu, but it was only now that I realized he was an extremist Hutu who had always hated Tutsis. *Extremist* . . . how I hated that word. Once again Buhoro made me feel ashamed of what God had made me—a Tutsi. I was so embarrassed and humiliated that I had to force myself to greet the other guests before retreating from the room in shame.

I was so relieved when I found Janet, my best friend since primary school, sitting in the dining room chatting with another girl. I rushed over and cried, "Janet! Oh, I'm so happy to see you. It's been so horrible for me these past few days; the world has gone crazy. People are being murdered all over the village, and we've been treated like dogs. . . . Thank God you're here! It's so good to see a friendly face."

I threw my arms around her, hugging her as tightly as I could, but her body stiffened. When I pulled back and looked into her face, it wasn't friendly at all—in fact, her eyes refused to meet mine.

She's in shock, I thought, suddenly concerned for her well-being. *What's wrong with me? I haven't even asked her how she is!*

"Aren't you feeling well, Janet? I haven't been sleeping either, but now we've found each other. My father told me to stay with Pastor Murinzi, but I'm not comfortable here. It's so lucky you're visiting! I'll come home with you, and we can keep each other company until things are back to normal."

Janet bent down, grabbed her purse, and stood up. "I don't know what you can be thinking, Immaculée," she said, still not looking at me. "I'm certainly not going to hide you, and neither will my father. We don't hide Tutsis in our home."

"But . . . Janet?"

She turned to the other girl and said, "I'm leaving," and then walked out of the house and never looked back.

I staggered into the hall and leaned against the wall. How could my dearest friend turn against me? We'd loved each other like sisters once—how could she be so cruel now? How was it possible for a heart to harden so quickly?

Augustine came up to me with Lechim, who was Pastor Murinzi's youngest son and the closest male friend I'd ever had. We'd known each other since primary school, and because he was great pals with Damascene, he was always hanging around our house. He'd joined our group of friends on outings and picnics over the years, and we'd developed crushes on each other. He even gave me my first kiss just before my 20th birthday, a kiss that was the beginning and end of our romance because we agreed not to tamper with our wonderful friendship. And now, because of that friendship, I was in a big house with a kind hand on my shoulder instead of in the fields being hunted by machete-carrying killers.

"Come on, Immaculée, don't be upset. Everyone is behaving strangely today," Lechim said sweetly, patting me tenderly. "Come on, I'll take you to my sister's room, and Augustine can stay in the boys' room. The girls will be good to you, Immaculée."

I was so happy that Lechim had found me, and I knew his sister Dusenge very well. Like him, she was a kind, good soul. I think that we might have gotten along so well because their mother, Elena, who had died a few years earlier, was Tutsi. Lechim and Dusenge were considered Hutu because that's what their father was—but because of their mom, they understood what it meant to be Tutsi in Rwanda.

As we were walking to the room, Augustine began crying. "I want to go home. I want to see my mother, my father, and my sister. I want to leave here and go to Kigali."

"Come on," I said, taking his hand. "Don't get like this. Be strong. You can't go anywhere right now—it's much too dangerous out there. Let's be grateful that we're safe. Besides, even if you look Tutsi, you *are* a Hutu and have your identity card to prove it. No one will harm you."

"No, Immaculée, you're wrong. I heard people whispering in the living room that I'm a member of the Tutsi rebel army. They think I'm spying on them for the RPF! My identity card doesn't mean a thing; they'll say it's a fake. Nobody around here knows who I am. They're going to kill me . . . I know they're going to kill me!" My young friend was so shaken up that tears ran down his cheeks and his hands trembled.

"Don't panic, Augustine. As long as we're together we can look out for each other and we'll be okay."

I don't know where I got the strength to say such things, since I was terrified and completely unsure if we'd survive. But I had to have faith that God would help us; otherwise, why would we endure all the suffering, anguish, and betrayal?

DUSENGE WASN'T IN HER ROOM, so I lay quietly with my eyes shut. I'd barely slept in days, but I still couldn't nod off. My mind drifted over the events that had led me to the pastor's house. I saw my family sitting around our radio not knowing what to do. I envisioned my mother's ashen face as she slept outside to protect me. I remembered my father standing in front of thousands of frightened people trying to encourage them. And I recalled the machetes in the killers' hands on the road to the pastor's.

As my thoughts swirled, I heard Damascene's excited voice and sat up with a start. I thought I'd been dreaming, but I wasn't. I definitely heard my brother talking to someone just outside the bedroom. A few seconds later, he was in the room with me.

"Damascene, what's happened? Where are Mom and Dad?"

"I don't know, Immaculée. We were separated, and they had to run away."

"Why? What happened?"

"They burned it down."

"What? Who burned what down?"

"The killers . . . they burned down our house. It's gone."

I sank back on the bed. My father had just finished our home, which he'd built for my mother with his own hands. It was to be their retirement castle, and seeing it destroyed would have broken his heart.

"Does Dad know about the house?"

"Of course he does—they burned it down in front of him," Damascene said. And then he proceeded to fill me in on everything that had happened at home in the few hours since I'd left. Apparently our father had refused to believe that the government was behind the killings, so he drove to see Mr. Kabayi, the burgomaster, to ask for protection.

"But Kabayi tried to starve Dad in prison," I interrupted. "What was he thinking?"

"He said that he had no choice," Damascene continued. "The killers were all around the house, and more kept coming. Dad felt responsible for the people who'd come to him for help, so he went to Kabayi to beg for protection. He told the burgomaster that there were thousands of Tutsis at our house and asked him to send as many soldiers as he could."

Damascene said that Mr. Kabayi told my father not to worry and sent two soldiers to escort him home. But everything turned ugly when they got there.

"The soldiers started mocking Dad. They laughed at him and asked, 'What kind of idiot are you? How stupid can you be, thinking that the burgomaster sent us to protect you and all the cockroaches? These cockroaches need to be exterminated!'"

At that point, Vianney came into the room. Both of my brothers had been traumatized: Damascene was pale, and Vianney's face had a hollow, haunted expression. Damascene's voice was strained as he told me what happened next.

"The soldiers fired their guns in the air to rally the killers . . . and the killers came running, screeching like animals and waving their machetes. The Tutsis who'd been staying near our house began screaming so loudly that it was like listening to a giant flock of screeching crows. They ran in all directions, thousands of them in total panic.

"Dad, Mom, and Vianney all backed away from the house. I followed them, making sure that the killers didn't charge at us. The soldiers turned to the killers and yelled, 'This house is full of cockroaches—fumigate it! What are you waiting for? You have a job to do! It's time to stomp these cockroaches!'

"That's when the killers went berserk. They broke into the house, smashed everything, and set fire to the car. Whatever they didn't smash, they looted . . . and then they torched the house. In less than five minutes, it was completely swallowed up by flames. Dad collapsed on the ground—he just passed out—he couldn't believe what he was seeing. He'd told people that things would get better, but now he saw that he was wrong, and that it was too late to do anything about it. His whole life was burning up in front of him.

"We helped him down the road to where he'd hidden his motorcycle, and he got on. He made Mom climb onto the seat behind him. Since the killers were going crazy, we didn't have time to talk, think, or even say good-bye. Dad yelled, 'Run! Go to Pastor Murinzi's and find your sister. I have to get your mother away from here. Hide—we'll find each other later!'

"Mom was crying into his shirt. She looked at us and said, 'My boys . . . what will become of my boys?' That's all I heard her saying over the motorcycle engine. Then they were gone."

"But where did they go?" I asked, heartbroken.

"I don't know—maybe to Aunt Cecile's house or to one of the churches for shelter. It was so confusing . . . we were in a stampede. Thousands and thousands of Tutsis were running for their lives— toward the mountains, the forest, the swamp, and the stadium. But Immaculée, I think that no matter where they go, there will be killers. They're everywhere, and now we don't even have a home to hide in."

I was speechless, but I felt as if I had to give my brothers something to look forward to. "Look, we lost our house, but our home will be wherever we are together," I said, with as much hopefulness as I could muster. "We'll all move to the city—we'll go to Kigali and start over."

Both of my brothers looked at me as though I were insane. "Immaculée, what are you thinking?" Damascene asked in irritation, sounding fed up with my optimism. "The killing is going on all around us. We passed dead bodies on the road coming here, and most of them are people we know! *We're trapped.*"

He looked at me with an expression I'd never seen on his face before. I didn't know what it was: accusation, disappointment, anger? And his next words stung like a whip: "Why did you keep telling us all along that things were going to be okay?"

A wave of guilt rolled over me. Had my optimism led my brothers and parents into this nightmare we were living in now? Was I responsible for their fate? What else could we have done, since Dad wouldn't leave, and everything had happened so fast? Should I have despaired, sunk into depression, or become hysterical over our plight? That would have made matters worse. People need hope to survive.

I refused to believe that God had made us Tutsis only to have us slaughtered. But here was Damascene, whom I loved so dearly, looking at me with anger and despair. "I'm sorry," I said through tears. "But all we have left is hope, so let's hold on to it. We can't give up yet. Remember, you promised to come to my graduation next year. We can make it through this."

"You really think so?" my brother asked, showing me his shining smile again, but sounding unconvinced.

I didn't know if we'd even make it through the night, but I summoned up all the conviction I could manage. "Sure, Damascene, we'll make it."

"Okay, I won't give up hope if you don't," he said, and turned to Vianney.

"You better stay with Augustine because he's very frightened. And whatever happens, *do not* leave this house—and don't let Immaculée leave. There are murderers and rapists everywhere. Promise me you'll do that."

"I promise," our baby brother said.

Then Damascene announced: "I'm not going to stay here. I know that the pastor doesn't like Dad, and I can tell he doesn't like me either. Besides, too many people saw me come here, and that may lead them to you."

I pleaded with him to stay with us, but he wouldn't change his mind. His good friend Bonn lived nearby, so Damascene said he was going to stay with him. Bonn was a Hutu, so he might be able to hide my brother for quite a while.

I walked Damascene to the porch, but it was too painful to talk to him. We'd never parted company without saying "See you soon" or "See you in a few weeks." Now I couldn't bring myself to say good-bye, knowing that this could be the last time I'd ever look at his beautiful face.

My brother, my soul mate, put his hands in mine, and they felt soft and light as feathers. No matter how hard I squeezed them, I couldn't feel the weight of his palms against mine—it was like holding the hands of a disappearing soul. My heart felt like it was exploding.

We stood staring at each other silently until Damascene gently pulled his hands away, smiled sadly, and stepped through the gate.

≫≪

CHAPTER 8

Farewell to the Boys

Not long after Damascene left, there was a knock on the pastor's front door. I heard the voice of Nzima, one of Vianney's high school teachers, asking for Pastor Murinzi. There was a muffled conversation, and then the door closed. I went out back and found Nzima sitting alone in the deep shadow of the pastor's shade tree. Even in the poor light, the pain on his face was easy to see.

He sounded like a frightened child: "What will they do? Do you think that they'll kill us?"

When I heard him at the door, I selfishly hoped that he'd be able to offer me words of comfort and give me strength, but it was he who desperately needed both.

Nzima told me that his wife and children were visiting his mother-in-law in a distant village. He had no way of knowing if they were safe, and he was tortured by the uncertainty. "I have visions I can't rid myself of," he said. "I see my wife and babies being slaughtered, cut up in front of me. And I can do nothing to stop it. For all I know, they're lying dead in the road right now."

I tried to console him as best I could, but what could I say? How many times could I tell someone that things were going to be okay when I wasn't sure what was going to happen myself?

He sighed deeply. "Where can I go? Everybody has a machete out there, and I saw others with guns."

"Stay here until the killing stops, and then you'll find your family," I said, hoping to buoy his spirits.

He shook his head and stood up. "I won't be staying here, and there's nowhere else for me to go, my child."

"I will pray for you."

"Thank you, Immaculée."

He said good-bye and walked to the front yard, where Pastor Murinzi was waiting. The pastor must have told Nzima that he couldn't stay because when he pointed to the gate, Nzima walked through it without saying a word. Later I heard that the poor man was hacked to death just a few hundred yards down the road from the pastor's house.

A couple of hours later, I was alone in a small bedroom when Pastor Murinzi quietly ushered five other Tutsi women in. I recognized all of them from the area but knew none of them well.

The pastor was agitated as he brought them into the room. "Hurry, hurry! You must hurry! And be quiet!" He was muttering so quickly and quietly that we barely heard him.

"Wait here, and keep quiet," he said, shutting the door behind him as he left.

And there we were, six Tutsi women who were virtually strangers to each other, except for two things we had in common: We were hunted, and we had nowhere else to hide. We stood looking at each other, too frightened to speak or even introduce ourselves. We didn't know what was happening outside, but judging from the pastor's nervousness, things were bad.

Suddenly there were screams outside the house—blood-curdling shrieks that made the hairs on our arms stand up.

Then the horrible, angry voices came, yelling, "Kill them! Kill them! Kill them all!"

There was more screaming and cries for help, followed by, "Kill him! Kill him! Kill him!"

We panicked. Several of the women dived to the floor and hid under the bed. I was trembling so hard that I thought the floor was shaking. My eyes scoured the room for a place to hide, zeroing in on a small crawl space in the ceiling.

"We can hide up there," I whispered, dragging a chair beneath the hole and scrambling up. I pulled another woman up, and together we hoisted the others through the hole. Then we waited for the pastor to return. We crouched in that cramped, stifling space until our clothes were soaked with sweat and we were gasping for air. Two hours later, Pastor Murinzi came back. He stood in the middle of the room and scratched his head with a stunned look on his face.

"Where are they? My God, I left them right here!"

I would have laughed if I wasn't so frightened. "We're up here!" I whispered, popping my head out of the hole.

The pastor shook his head, then told us to come down immediately so that he could talk to us. His face was still very troubled. "I know that you're all scared, and you should be," he said. "It's gotten out of control out there. The killers are going into *everyone's* homes. They haven't come inside mine today, but they could at any time. Honestly, I don't know what to do with you . . . I have to think it over."

He must have seen our panic, because he came up with a solution very quickly. "Don't worry, I won't turn you out," he assured us. "But you must listen very carefully. Early tomorrow morning, before anyone is awake, I will take you to another room, where you'll stay until the killing stops. I will tell everyone in the house that I have sent you away. I'll be the only one who knows you are here. Idle gossip could get us all killed. I've seen these killing sprees before—once the blood-lust is in the air, you can trust no one, not even your own children. If one person discovers you, you're finished! And by God, I don't want your blood in my house or on my hands."

Then the pastor turned to me and said words that cut me like a knife: "Your brother and his friend can't stay here. They must leave and fend for themselves. It's too dangerous for me to protect men. As it is, you women are already too many for me to hide."

He couldn't look me in the eye—we both knew that sending Vianney and Augustine away now would almost certainly mean delivering them to their deaths.

"Oh, no, Pastor Murinzi, please! You can't—"

He held his finger to his lips, ending the conversation. "They have to go, Immaculée. When I come to get you in a few hours, you will take them to the door and let them out. Be careful that no one sees you."

As the pastor left the room, I cursed him under my breath. How could he act like a saint by protecting us, then turn around and push my brother and Augustine into the arms of killers?

I didn't want to scorn the man who was saving us, but I couldn't help myself—I suspected the worst. In other killing sprees, some Hutu men had hidden Tutsi women while turning away Tutsi men. It was said that they hid Tutsi women because of their beauty, planning to claim them as their own after their menfolk were murdered. It was yet another way that Tutsis, especially Tutsi women, were brutalized. I began to think that the pastor had ulterior motives in taking in six women.

WE TRIED TO SLEEP THAT NIGHT, but it was difficult to rest when we had no clue as to what lay ahead. Every time I closed my eyes, I imagined Vianney and Augustine walking out of the house and into a frenzy of swinging machetes and screaming madmen. The boys were so young—only 20 and 18, respectively—how could I let them go out on their own? It would be a betrayal for me to let them leave.

I decided to go with them, but then changed my mind . . . and changed it again and again. How could I protect them if we were attacked? I might even slow them down. More attention would be drawn to them if they were with a woman, and that would get us all killed.

And then Damascene's parting words rang in my ears: "Don't leave this place, no matter what."

I groaned quietly, but it was loud enough to alarm the others.

"Don't worry, your brother is a grown man, not a little boy," said Therese, one of the ladies hiding with me, who'd been watching me toss and turn for an hour. "They're strong young men—they can take care of themselves. If you go with them, you'll bring the rapists to you. Let them go—it's the best thing. Trust me; I'm a mother. It's better for you to stay with us."

I thought that she was probably right, but it didn't make things any easier. I worried that if Vianney left, I might never see *anyone* in my family again.

Two hours before dawn, the pastor slipped into the room and woke us with a stern whisper. "Get up, let's go! Come on, hurry!" He looked at me and said, "Say good-bye to your brother, and then come right back."

Walking into that room and waking up Vianney and Augustine was the hardest thing I ever had to do. Tears poured down my face like rain—thank God the darkness hid the shame, sorrow, and unmistakable fear in my eyes.

I placed my hand on Vianney's back and woke him gently, speaking softly and slowly to control my sobbing. "Wake up . . . it's morning. The pastor says . . . we can't all stay . . . the men . . . you have to go . . . don't worry . . . you'll meet Daddy . . . he'll tell you what to do."

I felt wretched, as though my heart was being squeezed.

Vianney and Augustine jumped from the bed. "What? Go where, Immaculée? We can't go anywhere without Damascene. What will happen to him if we leave without him?" my little brother said, rubbing the sleep from his eyes.

His words tore at me. He was thinking of our brother's safety while I was sending him into danger. I felt like a mother throwing her baby to a pack of wolves. "Damascene will be okay," I said, trying to make my voice sound steady. "He is somewhere safe. Come on, we have to go."

I hustled the boys down the dark hall to the front door. I hugged Vianney as hard as I could and kissed him again and again. "Be strong, Vianney. We will meet again soon."

They walked out the door and were swallowed by the darkness.

≫≪

PART II

IN HIDING

CHAPTER 9

Into the Bathroom

I closed the door behind Vianney and Augustine and joined the other Tutsi women.

Pastor Murinzi carried a flashlight and led us down the dark hallway to his bedroom. Our eyes followed the beam of light along the walls until it landed on a door that I assumed opened to the yard.

"This is where you'll stay," he said, swinging the door open to reveal our new home: a small bathroom about four feet long and three feet wide. The light shimmered as it bounced off the white enamel tiles on the bottom half of the walls. There was a shower stall at one end and a toilet at the other—the room wasn't big enough for a sink. And there was a small air vent/window near the ceiling that was covered with a piece of red cloth, which somehow made the room feel even smaller.

I couldn't imagine how all six of us could possibly fit in this space, but the pastor herded us through the door and packed us in tight. "While you're in here, you must be absolutely quiet, and I mean *silent,*" he said. "If you make any noise, you will die. If they hear you, they will find you, and then they will kill you. No one must know that you're here, not even my children. Do you understand?"

"Yes, Pastor," we mumbled in unison.

"And don't flush the toilet or use the shower." He shone his light along the wall above the toilet. "There's another bathroom on the other side of that wall, which uses the same plumbing. So if you absolutely must flush, wait until you hear someone using the other bathroom, then do so at *exactly* the same time. Do you understand?"

"Yes, Pastor."

The flashlight clicked off, and his last words were spoken in the dark. "I think that they're going to keep killing for another week, maybe less. If you're careful, you might live through this. I'd hate for the killers to get you . . . I know what they would do."

He shut the door and left us standing in blackness, our bodies pressing against one another. The musky heat of our breath, sweat, and skin mingled together and made us feel faint.

We tried to sit, but there wasn't enough room for all of us to move at the same time. The four tallest had to push our backs against the wall and slide to the tile floor, then pull the smaller girls down on top of us. It was past 3 A.M. and we were all wide-awake, yet we didn't dare speak. We sat as best we could, listening to the crickets outside and to our own labored breathing.

I prayed silently, asking God to protect Vianney and Augustine and keep my parents and Damascene safe. I thanked Him for delivering us to the bathroom—I truly believed that God had guided Pastor Murinzi to bring us here, and for the first time in days, I felt safe. If *I* hadn't noticed the bathroom we were currently in after so many visits to the house, no one else would.

I asked God to bless Pastor Murinzi for risking his own safety to help us . . . but then I winced at the prayer. A flush of anger burned my cheeks as I remembered how he'd sent my brother and our friend into the night. I prayed that God would eventually help me forgive the pastor.

The moon emerged from behind a cloud, and a thin streak of pale light slipped through a crack in the red curtain, providing enough illumination for me to make out the faces of my companions. Sitting beside me was Athanasia, a pretty, dark-skinned 14-year-old with big beautiful eyes that caught the moonlight. Sitting on top of her was 12-year-old Beata, still wearing her school uniform, who looked lost and very frightened. I pulled her onto my lap, cradling her in my arms until she closed her eyes.

Across from me was Therese, who, at 55, was the eldest of the group. She wore a colorful, traditional Rwandan wrap-dress popular with married women. She looked more worried than any of us, probably because she only had two of her six children—Claire and Sanda—with her. Claire was very light-skinned, and even though she was my age, she was nervous and withdrawn and wouldn't make eye contact. Her little sister Sanda was only seven, and the youngest of the group. She was cute, sweet, and surprisingly calm. She never once cried or looked frightened, even when the rest of us were trembling—I think she must have been in shock the entire time we were in that bathroom.

The pastor's repeated warnings to be quiet had burned into us. We sat in an uncomfortable heap, too afraid to adjust our positions or to even breathe too heavily. We waited for the gray light of dawn to fill the room, then carefully pried ourselves apart to take turns standing and stretching. A two- or three-minute break was all we allowed ourselves before resuming our awkward positions on the floor.

When morning broke, the birds in the pastor's shade tree began singing. I was jealous of them, thinking, *How lucky you are to have been born birds and have freedom—after all, look at what we humans are doing to ourselves.*

WE WERE SO EXHAUSTED, HUNGRY, CRAMPED, AND HOT that our first day in the bathroom passed in a painful haze. It was impossible to sleep—if I dozed off, I was immediately awoken by a leg cramp or someone's elbow knocking against my ribs.

In the early evening, we heard Pastor Murinzi talking to someone outside. "No, no, no," he said. "I don't know what you're talking about—I'm a good Hutu, and I'd never hide Tutsis. There are no Tutsis here . . . they left last night."

We stared at each other with our eyes wide open. We were terrified.

"I don't want any trouble with the government," the pastor continued. "You people know me, and you should protect this house . . . those Tutsi rebels might attack me for being such a good Hutu."

Whoever the pastor was talking to left, and we relaxed. Pastor Murinzi had just lied to save us—I felt assured that he wouldn't hand us over to the killers. He had little choice now, because if he turned us in, the killers would know that he'd hidden us. They'd call him a moderate, a traitor to his tribe, and would kill him as surely as they'd kill us.

I breathed easier and hugged young Beata, who was lying across my lap. I remembered how my mother sometimes held me in her lap when I was young and frightened. The memory of Mom saddened me—this was the first time in my life that I didn't know the whereabouts of my parents or brothers. I slipped into a half sleep and dreamed of Vianney, Augustine, and Damascene knocking on the pastor's gate, while behind them, our house was burning. I saw my parents sitting on Dad's motorcycle, and my mother asking, "What will happen to my boys?"

While I was dreaming, Pastor Murinzi opened the door, and without saying a word, shoved a plate of cold potatoes and beans into the room. It was late, maybe 11 P.M., and none of us had had anything to eat or drink for nearly two days.

We attacked the plate, grabbing the food with our dirty fingers and stuffing it into our mouths.

When the pastor returned five minutes later with forks, we'd already devoured every bit of food. He stared at the plate, and then looked at us with pity. A moment later he tossed a very thin mattress into the room. "You've traveled down a long road. Now try to get some rest," he said, and closed the door.

WHEN WE AWOKE THE NEXT DAY, WE TOOK TURNS stretching our aching muscles. Moving even an inch was a major production because we couldn't talk to one another. We quickly worked out forms of sign language that would become our silent shorthand for the remainder of our stay in the bathroom.

I grimaced at the pain in my cramped legs, thinking that I'd have quite a tale of hardship to tell after the war. "Listen to what I had to endure," I'd boast to my friends. "I spent an entire day and night trapped in a tiny bathroom with five strangers. What a hero I am!"

No sooner had I begun my little fantasy than I was jolted back to reality by images of my family: my parents fleeing our burning house, Damascene slipping sadly away, and Vianney and Augustine wandering in the open with nowhere to hide. Thank God that Aimable was safely away from Rwanda in another country! But what about the thousands of displaced Tutsis who had sought refuge at our house? What had become of them? Had they found shelter, or were they lying somewhere bleeding to death? I felt silly and selfish for indulging in my self-pity when thousands were undoubtedly suffering far more.

It was my turn to stretch when a commotion erupted outside. There were dozens, maybe hundreds, of voices, some yelling, others chanting. We knew immediately that the killers had arrived.

"Let us hunt them in the forests, lakes, and hills; let us find them in the church; let us wipe them from the face of the earth!"

I stood on my tiptoes and peeked out the window through a little hole in the curtain. The other ladies grabbed at me, trying to pull me down. Athanasia shook her head wildly, silently mouthing, "Get down! They're looking for us! Get down before they see you!"

I ignored them, knocking their hands away and peering through the hole. I immediately regretted my decision because I was petrified by what I saw.

Hundreds of people surrounded the house, many of whom were dressed like devils, wearing skirts of tree bark and shirts of dried banana leaves, and some even had goat horns strapped onto their heads. Despite their demonic costumes, their faces were easily recognizable, and there was murder in their eyes.

They whooped and hollered. They jumped about, waving spears, machetes, and knives in the air. They chanted a chilling song of genocide while doing a dance of death: "Kill them, kill them, kill them all; kill them big and kill them small! Kill the old and kill the young . . . a baby snake is still a snake, kill it, too, let none escape! Kill them, kill them, kill them all!"

It wasn't the soldiers who were chanting, nor was it the trained militiamen who had been tormenting us for days. No, these were my neighbors, people I'd grown up and gone to school with—some had even been to our house for dinner.

I spotted Kananga, a young man I'd known since childhood. He was a high school dropout my dad had tried to help straighten out. I saw Philip, a young man who'd been too shy to look anyone in the eye, but who now seemed completely at home in this group of killers. At the front of the pack I could make out two local schoolteachers who were friends of Damascene. I recognized dozens of Mataba's most prominent citizens in the mob, all of whom were in a killing frenzy, ranting and screaming for Tutsi blood. The killers leading the group pushed their way into the pastor's house, and suddenly the chanting was coming from all directions.

"Find them, find them, kill them all!"

My head was spinning; I fell backward onto the ladies. I couldn't breathe. "Dear God, save us . . . " I whispered, but couldn't remember the words to any of my prayers. A wave of despair washed over me, and I was overwhelmed by fear.

That's when the devil first whispered in my ear. *Why are you calling on God? Look at all of them out there . . . hundreds of them looking for you. They are legion, and you are one. You can't possibly survive—you* won't *survive. They're inside the house, and they're moving through the rooms. They're close, almost here . . . they're going to find you, rape you, cut you, kill you!*

My heart was pounding. What was this voice? I squeezed my eyes shut as tightly as I could to resist the negative thoughts. I grasped the red and white rosary my father had given me, and silently prayed with all my might: *God, in the Bible You said that You can do anything for anybody. Well, I am one of those anybodies, and I need You to do something for me now. Please, God, blind the killers when they reach the pastor's bedroom—don't let them find the bathroom door, and don't let them see us! You saved Daniel in the lions' den, God, You stopped the lions from ripping him apart . . . stop these killers from ripping us apart, God! Save us, like You saved Daniel!*

I prayed more intensely than I'd ever prayed before, but still the negative energy wracked my spirit. The voice of doubt was in my ear again as surely as if Satan himself were sitting on my shoulder. I literally felt the fear pumping through my veins, and my blood was on fire. *You're going to die, Immaculée!* the voice taunted. *You compare yourself to Daniel? How conceited you are . . . Daniel was pure of heart and loved by God—he was a prophet, a saint! What are you? You are nothing . . . you deserve suffering and pain . . . you deserve to die!*

I clutched my rosary as though it were a lifeline to God. In my mind and heart I cried out to Him for help: *Yes, I am nothing, but You are forgiving. I am human and I am weak, but please, God, give me Your forgiveness. Forgive my trespasses . . . and* please *send these killers away before they find us!*

My temples pounded. The dark voice was in my head, filling it with fearful, unspeakable images. *Dead bodies are everywhere. Mothers have seen their babies chopped in half, their fetuses ripped from their wombs . . . and you think you should be spared? Mothers prayed for God to spare their babies and He ignored them—why should He save you when innocent babies are being murdered? You are selfish, and you have no shame. Listen, Immaculée . . . do you hear them? The killers are outside your door—they're here for you.*

My head was burning, but I did hear the killers in the hall, screaming, "Kill them! Kill them all!"

No! God is love, I told the voice. *He loves me and wouldn't fill me with fear. He will not abandon me. He will not let me die cowering on a bathroom floor. He will not let me die in shame!*

I struggled to form an image of God in my mind, envisioning two pillars of brilliant white light burning brightly in front of me, like two giant legs. I wrapped my arms around the legs, like a frightened child clinging to its mother. I begged God to fill me with His light and strength, to cast out the dark energy from my heart: *I'm holding on to Your legs, God, and I do not doubt that You can save me. I will not let go of You until You have sent the killers away.*

The struggle between my prayers and the evil whispers that I was sure belonged to the devil raged in my mind. I never stopped praying . . . and the whispering never relented.

IN THE EVENING, THE PASTOR OPENED THE DOOR and found us all in a sort of trance. I was bathed in sweat, exhausted, clutching my rosary in both hands, and oblivious to my surroundings. I was still mouthing prayer after prayer while staring vacantly at the others. Therese was using one hand to cover her eyes and the other to hold her Bible firmly on top of her head. And young Beata was crouching on her knees, arms in front of her, hands clasped in prayer.

The pastor called our names, but not one of us heard him. Finally, he shook us to awaken us from our stupor. I looked up at him, blinking, confused, and completely taken aback when he began laughing at us.

"What are you ladies doing? For heaven's sake, relax. The killers left seven hours ago. I can't believe you're all still praying."

To me, those seven hours had passed in what seemed like a few minutes, yet I was utterly drained. In all my years of praying, I'd never focused so completely on God, or been so keenly aware of the presence of darkness. I'd seen evil in the eyes of the killers, and had felt evil all around me while the house was being searched. And I'd listened to the dark voice, letting it convince me that we were about to be slaughtered. Every time I succumbed to my fear and believed the lies of that poisonous whispering, I felt as though the skin were being peeled from my scalp. It was only by focusing on God's positive energy that I was able to pull myself through that first visit by the killers. My father had always said that you could never pray too much . . . now I could see that he was right.

I realized that my battle to survive this war would have to be fought inside of me. Everything strong and good in me—my faith, hope, and courage—was vulnerable to the dark energy. If I lost my faith, I knew that I wouldn't be able to survive. I could rely only on God to help me fight.

The visit by the killers had left us all spent. Pastor Murinzi brought us a plate of food, but despite our hunger, we were too tired to eat. The food was untouched when he returned around midnight.

The pastor returned again in the middle of the night during a heavy storm. The rain beat down so loudly against the iron roof that he was able to talk freely without the fear of being overheard. "We were lucky today. They searched all over the house and looked in every room. They looked in the yard and dug through the dung heap behind the cow pen. They crawled into the ceiling and under the furniture—they even stuck their machetes into my suitcases to make sure that I wasn't hiding Tutsi babies. They were crazed, like rabid animals. Their eyes were glazed and red . . . I think they'd been smoking drugs.

"But when they reached my bedroom, they saw that it was neat, so they didn't want to mess it up. They said that they'd leave the bedroom for now but warned that they'd search it next time when they came back."

"Next time!" we gasped.

I couldn't imagine reliving the same ordeal. Surely God wouldn't put us through that suffering twice!

"You never know when they're going to come back," the pastor said. "They could come at any time, and God help us all if they find you."

His parting sentence echoed in my mind, keeping me awake all night and throughout the next day.

Pastor Murinzi returned the next evening in a panic. "A friend told me that the leader of a death squad thinks the killers did a bad job searching the house yesterday," he hissed. "Some of you were seen in the house a few days ago, and there are rumors that you're hiding here. A different group of killers is being sent to search more thoroughly."

I moaned as my body went limp. I simply didn't have the strength to live through another of the killers' hunting expeditions. *God, why don't You just lead them to us now and get it over with?* I entreated. *Why do You let us suffer like this? Why do You torture us?*

How could we escape again? The house that once seemed so huge had become my cell, a death trap. I could think of only one escape: I wanted to go to heaven. *Oh, God,* I prayed soundlessly, *I have no heart left to fight. I'm ready to give up . . . please give me strength and protect me from the demons that are all around me. Show me how to make the killers blind again.*

I raised my head and opened my eyes. When I saw the pastor standing in the doorway, a crystal clear image flashed through my mind. "I have an idea," I told him in a hushed but insistent voice. "Can you push your wardrobe in front of the bathroom door? It's tall and wide enough to completely cover it, so if the killers can't see the door, they'll never find us. It will be as though they're blind!"

Pastor Murinzi thought for a moment and then shook his head. "No, it wouldn't change anything; in fact, it would probably make matters worse. If they look behind the wardrobe and find the door, they will be even more vicious with you."

"Oh, no! Pastor, please, you must . . ." I was certain that God had sent me a sign. In my soul, I knew that if the wardrobe were in front of the door, we'd be saved. But the pastor was immovable, so I did something I'd never done in my life: I got on my knees and bowed down to him. "Please, I'm begging you," I said. "I know in my heart that if you don't put the wardrobe in front of the door, they're going to find us the next time they search. Don't worry about making them angry—they can only kill us once. Please do this for us . . . God will reward you if you do."

I don't know if it was the sight of me begging on my knees or the fear that I'd be overheard that convinced him, but he relented. "All right, all right. Keep your voice down, Immaculée. I'll move it right now. I hope it helps, but I doubt it will."

He disappeared, and a moment later we heard the wardrobe sliding in front of the bathroom door. The other ladies looked at me and whispered, "That was such a good idea—what put it into your head?"

I couldn't remember if I'd ever seen the pastor's wardrobe before, but I knew for certain that the idea to move it came to me when I prayed for help.

"God," I simply replied.

※※

CHAPTER 10

Confronting My Anger

Several days passed in relative calm. Only occasionally did we hear the killers outside, singing their sick songs. We prayed silently throughout the day and communicated with each other through sign language. Every 12 hours or so, we allowed ourselves a few precious moments of stretching. Other than that, we kept our movements to an absolute minimum, sitting in the same positions day and night.

We flushed the toilet according to Pastor Murinzi's orders—only when someone else in the house flushed the other one. Using the toilet was a challenge: We had so little room that one of us always had to sit on top of it, so when one of us had to relieve ourselves, we all had to shift position. That put us in danger of making noise and being discovered.

Oddly, in all the time that we were in the bathroom, I can't recall actually seeing someone else use the toilet, even though it was in the middle of our little space, nor do I recall being bothered by any odors. Our menstrual cycles came, one after the other, and we perplexed the pastor with constant requests for more toilet paper. None of us were embarrassed by the situation, though—we learned to ignore these functions and forego the luxury of privacy, especially since it all seemed rather trivial in comparison to staying alive.

We ate whenever the pastor showed up with food, which was sporadically. Some days he didn't come until 3 or 4 A.M.; other days he didn't come at all. (He slid the wardrobe away from the door each time he needed to see us or bring us food, but he was always extremely careful not to be heard. There was a rug beneath the wardrobe that muffled the sound of the movement, so again, God was looking out for us.) Worried that someone would notice if he cooked extra food, he brought us his children's table scraps or whatever the servants tossed into the garbage. Sometimes, no matter how hungry we were, we couldn't bring ourselves to eat because what he gave us looked like pig food. (I laughed at myself, thinking about what a fussy eater I'd been at home.) Thankfully, he also brought us water to drink.

It seemed impossible, but after a few days of quiet we let our guard down a little. The pastor snapped us back to reality.

He came in one night and told us that the killers were nearby, going from house to house, ransacking homes, and killing every Tutsi they found. "They may come here in a few minutes, or they may not come until tomorrow or the next day. But they will definitely be back, so keep quiet," he warned us.

Any fantasy we had of finding some peace of mind in that bathroom evaporated. Our anxiety about the killers' return was constant mental and physical torture. I felt as if someone were stinging me with a cattle prod whenever the floor creaked or a dog barked. Since we could only sleep for brief periods at a time, my skin soon became dry and flaky, and I had a constant headache.

The mental anguish was even more intense. I was trapped alone with my thoughts, and the dark fears and doubts that had haunted me since my arrival became relentless—they wormed into my heart and undermined the foundation of my faith. When the killers were out of earshot, my thoughts drifted away from God, and the negative energy rushed in. Yet whenever I prayed, I immediately felt His love around me, and the anxiety eased.

So I resolved to pray during every waking moment, beginning as soon as my eyes opened at 4 or 5 A.M. My first prayer was always to thank God that the pastor's home had been built so it could shelter us during the genocide. Then I thanked Him for having the architect design the house with an extra bathroom, and for prompting the pastor to buy a wardrobe of exactly the right dimensions to conceal our hiding place.

After my warm-up devotions of thanks, I began praying my rosary. I prayed many different Catholic prayers on the red and white beads. Sometimes I prayed so intensely that I broke out in a sweat. Hours would pass. . . . When I finished the rosary and my prayers, I'd take a "break" to meditate on some of my favorite Bible passages.

Because I felt that my faith was under attack, I spent hours contemplating two verses I'd memorized from Mark, which talked about the power of faith. First, there was this one: "Therefore I say unto you, what things soever ye desire, when ye pray, believe that ye receive them, and ye shall have them" (Mark 11:24).

Then I would reflect on the other one: "For verily I say unto you, that whosoever shall say unto this mountain, be thou removed, and be thou cast into the sea; and shall not doubt in his heart, but shall believe that those things which he saith shall come to pass; he shall have whatsoever he saith" (Mark 11:23).

Even a few minutes not spent in prayer or contemplation of God became an invitation for Satan to stab me with his double-edged knife of doubt and self-pity. Prayer became my armor, and I wrapped it tightly around my heart.

THE PASTOR WAS ALWAYS AFRAID THAT WE'D SLIP UP and make noise, so he rarely let anyone into his bedroom. But sometimes, when one of his kids or servants would visit him there, we'd be on pins and needles until they left. About a week after we arrived, we heard the pastor talking to his son Sembeba.

"What do you make of all this killing, Dad? Don't you think that it's good—exactly what we Hutus should be doing? I mean, they taught us in school that hundreds of years ago the Tutsis did the same thing to us, so they deserve what they get, right?"

"Sembeba, you don't know what you're talking about. Leave me now. I want to sleep," the pastor replied.

"Those Tutsis have always thought they're superior . . . always looking down on us Hutus. Don't you think that if they were still in power today they'd be killing *us* right now? So killing them is self-defense, isn't it?"

His voice was so loud that I could tell that Sembeba was standing right beside the wardrobe, and I was terrified that he'd notice it had been moved. But as fearful as I was, I had to fight the urge to stand up and yell at him—his words made me so angry.

I knew that he wasn't entirely to blame for his ignorance because he'd learned his contempt for Tutsis in school . . . the same school I went to! Young Hutus were taught from an early age that Tutsis were inferior and not to be trusted, and they didn't belong in Rwanda. Hutus witnessed the segregation of Tutsis every day, first in the school-yard and then in the workplace, and they were taught to dehumanize us by calling us "snakes" and "cockroaches." No wonder it was so easy for them to kill us—snakes were to be killed and cockroaches exterminated!

The world had seen the same thing happen many times before. After it happened in Nazi Germany, all the big, powerful countries swore, "Never again!" But here we were, six harmless females huddled in darkness, marked for execution because we were born Tutsi. How had history managed to repeat itself? How had this evil managed to surface once again? Why had the devil been allowed to walk among us unchallenged, poisoning hearts and minds until it was too late?

The pastor must have known that we could hear this conversation because he scolded his son: "You are a stupid, stupid boy, Sembeba. There is never an excuse to shed blood without a very good reason. Now get out of my room. I'm sick of listening to you speak."

"You think *I'm* stupid for hating Tutsis, Father? Don't you think it's more stupid to hide them? I hope you know that that's what people say you're doing. Is it true? Are you hiding Tutsis in the house?"

My heart jumped into my mouth. My anger vanished, and once again, all I felt was fear.

"I've had enough of your foolishness, Sembeba. I'm not hiding any Tutsis. And it pains me to hear your vindictive words—your own mother was a Tutsi! I hope you know that your aunts, uncles, and all of your cousins are being hunted and killed. Now get out of my room and don't come back. *Get out!*"

We hadn't recovered from Sembeba's awful visit when we suddenly heard grenades exploding nearby. There was a series of terrific crashes that sounded like buildings collapsing. After each crash, we heard singing: "Kill them big, kill them small, kill them, kill them, kill them all!"

There was gunfire near the house, and the singing got so loud that we knew the killers were moving in our direction. I said a silent prayer, and moments later, we heard a clap of thunder, followed by a heavy downpour of rain. I can only guess that the killers ran back to their homes to stay dry, because all we heard for the rest of the night was the rain pounding against the metal roof.

That night the pastor came to us. His face was pale, and his eyes were bloodshot and weary. I thought that he was worried about Sembeba's suspicions, but it was much worse. He'd been walking about outside and had witnessed the depth of the horror unfolding around us. He told us that Interahamwe militiamen, soldiers, and Hutu civilians were destroying every Tutsi home they came across.

"It is very bad outside," he said, "very, very bad. I saw the killings in 1959 and 1973, and they were nothing compared to this. You have to understand that everything else has stopped—the schools and markets are closed, and people aren't going to work. The country has been shut down until the job is done."

"What do you mean 'until the job is done'? Until *what* job is done?" I asked.

The pastor paused. "Killing Tutsis. The job won't be done until all the Tutsis are dead. That's the government's main goal, and they're making everyone work very hard to achieve it. I have seen things today that I wish I had never seen."

My stomach twisted in a knot. I thought of my family, and I wanted to plug my ears and block out the pastor's voice.

"They have killed thousands of people," he continued, "tens of thousands . . . maybe hundreds of thousands, who knows? So many Tutsis ran into the churches for protection that the doors wouldn't close. Churches have always been off-limits for killing, but not this time. The killers burned the churches with the people still inside, and they shot anyone who tried to escape."

"Oh, God, no," I said. "On the radio they told everyone to go to the churches and stadiums for protection!"

"They might have said that, but it wasn't to protect anyone. The killers were sent there with machine guns and grenades. The bodies are piled up as high as my house . . . the stench is unbearable."

"Please, Pastor, enough! Don't say any more," I begged.

I wanted to ask him for news of my family, but I didn't want to hear what he might say. I couldn't bear to hear another word.

"I'm sorry to tell you these things, but you must know what's happening," he said. "You may very well be the only Tutsis left alive in all of Rwanda. If you saw what I've seen today, I don't think you would want to live."

The other ladies were crying, but not me. At that moment I had no tears to shed. I didn't feel sorrow; I felt anger. I was angrier than I'd ever been before—more than I believed was even possible. I was angry at the pastor for telling us such horrific details when our families were out there with nowhere to hide. I was angry at the government for unleashing this holocaust. I was angry at the rich countries for not stopping the slaughter. But most of all, I was angry at the Hutus—all of them. And as the pastor droned on about the horrible things being done to Tutsis, my anger grew into a deep, burning hatred.

I'd never done anything violent to anyone before, but at that moment I wished I had a gun so that I could kill every Hutu I saw. No, not a gun . . . I needed a machine gun, grenades, a flamethrower! I wanted to kill everyone, even Tutsis . . . I wanted to be like Rambo and set the whole country on fire. If I'd had an atomic bomb, I would have dropped it on Rwanda and killed everyone in our stupid, hateful land.

I looked at the pastor, and I wanted to kill him, too. I never would have believed that I would have had such capacity for rage, and I knew that I'd have to do a lot of praying to rid myself of it.

Pastor Murinzi finished talking, and we just sat there, looking up at him and waiting for more horrible news. It would have been kinder if he'd picked up a whip and beaten us to death. I couldn't accept his words without confirmation. As he left, I asked him to turn on the radio in his room so that we could listen to news reports. He agreed and shut the door.

A few minutes later we heard a government minister speaking on the national radio station: "I am appealing to all Hutus in Rwanda . . . it's time to stand together to fight our common enemy. Let's put aside political differences and defend ourselves. These Tutsi snakes are trying to kill us . . . we must kill them first. Kill the Tutsis wherever you find them—don't spare a single one. Kill the very old and kill the babies—they're all snakes. If the RPF rebels come back to our country, let them find only the corpses of their families. I urge all Hutus to do your duty and kill all our Tutsi enemies."

Now I knew for certain that the pastor hadn't been lying. I also knew that my father had been wrong to trust the government. The people he believed in had planned the genocide and were now calling on ordinary Rwandans to make it happen. There is a culture of obedience in Rwanda, and I knew that when many otherwise peaceful Hutus heard their leaders on the radio telling them to kill Tutsis, they'd dutifully pick up their machetes.

About an hour later, the pastor tuned in to the BBC news, and we heard a report saying that the RPF (the Tutsi rebel soldiers) had successfully fought their way from the far north of the country down to the capital, Kigali. The report said that the extremist Hutu government behind the genocide was in danger of collapsing. That news made our hearts leap—if the RPF reached Kigali, they should be able to fight their way south to our province in a few weeks! Sooner or later, they'd reach our little village and rescue us.

I just hoped that it was sooner, as later would probably be too late for us.

>>-<<

CHAPTER 11

Struggling to Forgive

I was deep in prayer when the killers came to search the house a second time.

It was past noon, and I'd been praying the rosary since dawn for God to give His love and forgiveness to all the sinners in the world. But try as I might, I couldn't bring myself to pray for the killers. That was a problem for me because I knew that God expected us to pray for *everyone,* and more than anything, I wanted God on my side.

As a compromise, I prayed the rosary multiple times, as intensely as I could, every day. Working through all those Hail Marys and Our Fathers took 12 or 13 hours—and whenever I reached the part of the Lord's Prayer that calls us to "forgive those who trespass against us," I tried not to think of the killers, because I knew that I couldn't forgive them.

During that second search, the killers' racket reached the edge of my prayers like an angry voice waking me from a dream. Then I heard four or five loud bangs next to my head, and they had my full attention. I realized that they were right there in the pastor's bedroom! They were rummaging through his belongings, ripping things from the wall, lifting up the bed, and overturning chairs.

"Look in that!" one of them yelled. "Now look under here. Move that chest! *Search everything!*"

I covered my mouth with my hands, fearing that they'd hear me breathing. They were only inches from my head . . . they were in front of the wardrobe—*the wardrobe!* I thanked God again for it, but my heart still thumped against my chest.

I could hear them *laughing*. They were having fun while going about killing people! I cursed them, wishing that they'd burn in hell.

The wardrobe banged against the door. I covered my ears and prayed: *God, please. You put the wardrobe there . . . now keep it there! Don't let them move it. Save us, Lord!*

My scalp was burning, and the ugly whispering slithered in my head again: *Why are you calling on God? Don't you have as much hatred in your heart as the killers do? Aren't you as guilty of hatred as they are? You've wished them dead; in fact, you wished that you could kill them yourself! You even prayed that God would make them suffer and make them burn in hell.*

I could hear the killers on the other side of the door, and entreated, *God, make them go away . . . save us from—*

Don't call on God, Immaculée, the voice broke in. *He knows that you're a liar. You lie every time you pray to Him to say that you love Him. Didn't God create us all in His image? How can you love God but hate so many of His creations?*

My thoughts were paralyzed. I knew that the demon in my head was right—I *was* lying to God every time I prayed to Him. I was so overwhelmed with hatred for the people responsible for the genocide that I had a hard time breathing.

At least 40 or 50 men were in the pastor's bedroom by this time, and they were shouting and jeering. They sounded drunk and mean, and their chanting was more vicious than usual: "Kill the Tutsis big and small . . . kill them one and kill them all. *Kill them!*"

I began praying, asking God to keep them away from the wardrobe and out of the house altogether.

Beneath the raucous singing, the dark voice taunted me: *It's no use . . . don't call on God. Who do you think sent the killers here for you? He did! Nothing can save you. God doesn't save liars.*

I began to pray for the killers and then stopped. I desperately wanted God's protection, but I believed in my heart that they deserved to die. I couldn't pretend that they hadn't slaughtered and raped thousands of people—I couldn't ignore the awful, evil things that they'd done to so many innocent souls.

Why do You expect the impossible from me? I asked God. *How can I forgive people who are trying to kill me, people who may have already slaughtered my family and friends? It isn't logical for me to forgive these killers. Let me pray for their victims instead, for those who've been raped and murdered and mutilated. Let me pray for the orphans and widows . . . let me pray for justice. God, I will ask You to punish those wicked men, but I cannot forgive them—I just can't.*

Finally, I heard the killers leaving. First they left the bedroom, then the house, and soon they were walking away down the road, their singing fading in the distance.

I resumed my prayers. I thanked God for saving us and for giving me the idea to put the wardrobe in front of the bathroom door. *That was so smart of You, God. You are very smart,* I said mentally, and thanked Him again. I wondered where the killers were off to, then I started praying for my friends and family: *Please look over my mother, God; she worries so much about us. Watch over my father; he can be so stubborn. . . .*

It was no use—my prayers felt hollow. A war had started in my soul, and I could no longer pray to a God of love with a heart full of hatred.

I tried again, praying for Him to forgive the killers, but deep down I couldn't believe that they deserved it at all. It tormented me . . . I tried to pray for them myself, but I felt like I was praying for the devil. *Please open my heart, Lord, and show me how to forgive. I'm not strong enough to squash my hatred—they've wronged us all so much . . . my hatred is so heavy that it could crush me. Touch my heart, Lord, and show me how to forgive.*

I struggled with the dilemma for hours on end. I prayed late into the night, all through the next day, and the day after that, and the day after that. I prayed all week, scarcely taking food or water. I couldn't remember when or for how long I'd slept, and was only vaguely aware of time passing.

ONE NIGHT I HEARD SCREAMING NOT FAR FROM THE HOUSE, and then a baby crying. The killers must have slain the mother and left her infant to die in the road. The child wailed all night; by morning, its cries were feeble and sporadic, and by nightfall, it was silent. I heard dogs snarling nearby and shivered as I thought about how that baby's life had ended. I prayed for God to receive the child's innocent soul, and then asked Him, *How can I forgive people who would do such a thing to an infant?*

I heard His answer as clearly as if we'd been sitting in the same room chatting: *You are all my children . . . and the baby is with Me now.*

It was such a simple sentence, but it was the answer to the prayers I'd been lost in for days.

The killers were like children. Yes, they were barbaric creatures who would have to be punished severely for their actions, but they were still children. They were cruel, vicious, and dangerous, as kids sometimes can be, but nevertheless, they were children. They saw, but didn't understand the terrible harm they'd inflicted. They'd blindly hurt others without thinking, they'd hurt their Tutsi brothers and sisters, they'd hurt God—and they didn't understand how badly they were hurting themselves. Their minds had been infected with the evil that had spread across the country, but their *souls* weren't evil. Despite their atrocities, they were children of God, and I could forgive a child, although it would not be easy . . . especially when that child was trying to kill me.

In God's eyes, the killers were part of His family, deserving of love and forgiveness. I knew that I couldn't ask God to love me if I were unwilling to love His children. At that moment, I prayed for the killers, for their sins to be forgiven. I prayed that God would lead them to recognize the horrific error of their ways before their life on Earth ended—before they were called to account for their mortal sins.

I held on to my father's rosary and asked God to help me, and again I heard His voice: *Forgive them; they know not what they do.*

I took a crucial step toward forgiving the killers that day. My anger was draining from me—I'd opened my heart to God, and He'd touched it with His infinite love. For the first time, I pitied the killers. I asked God to forgive their sins and turn their souls toward His beautiful light.

That night I prayed with a clear conscience and a clean heart. For the first time since I entered the bathroom, I slept in peace.

≫≪

CHAPTER 12

No Friends to Turn To

I found a place in the bathroom to call my own: a small corner of my heart. I retreated there as soon as I awoke, and stayed there until I slept. It was my sacred garden, where I spoke with God, meditated on His words, and nurtured my spiritual self.

When I meditated, I touched the source of my faith and strengthened the core of my soul. While horror swirled around me, I found refuge in a world that became more welcoming and wonderful with each visit. Even as my body shriveled, my soul was nourished through my deepening relationship with God.

I entered my special space through prayer; once inside, I prayed nonstop, using my rosary as an anchor to focus my thoughts and energies on God. The rosary beads helped me concentrate on the gospels and keep the words of God alive in my mind. I prayed in silence, but always mouthed the words to convince myself that I was really saying them . . . otherwise, doubt would creep in and the negative energy would come calling.

I spent hours contemplating the meaning of a single word, such as *forgiveness, faith,* or *hope.* I spent days with the word *surrender,* and I came to understand what it meant to surrender one's self to a Higher Power. I gave myself over completely to God. When I wasn't praying, I felt that I was no longer living in His light, and the world of the bathroom was too bleak to endure.

Toward the end of our first month in hiding, Pastor Murinzi came to us late one night with a plate of scraps. He'd acted with compassion when he took us in, but that seemed to be waning. On this night, his face was set in a scowl instead of its usual expression of concern and pity. "Your father was a very bad Tutsi!" he snapped at me.

"What? What do you mean?" I was taken completely off guard, not so much by the attack on my father as by the fact that the pastor referred to Dad in the past tense. I refused to acknowledge the possibility that any member of my family could be dead. "My father is a good *man,* Pastor—maybe the best man I ever met!"

"No, Immaculée, he was a bad Tutsi *and* a bad man . . . he was helping the RPF rebels plan a civil war." He looked at the other ladies, pointed at me, and said, "If they catch you and kill you, it will be because of Immaculée. The killers are hunting for her because of her father's activities." He was glaring at me, and I could feel the eyes of the other women on me.

"They found 600 guns in your house," he continued, turning back to me. "They also found grenades and a death list of Hutu names. That's the reason you Tutsis are being hunted and killed. If Hutus hadn't acted first, we'd be the ones being killed by Tutsis now!"

I couldn't believe what he was saying. The poisoned lies that the extremist Hutus were spreading had robbed Pastor Murinzi of his reason. He'd been friends with my father for years and knew that he'd dedicated himself to improving the lives of the poor and less fortunate. Dad had built schools and chapels for Tutsis, Hutus, and Twas alike, so how could the pastor accuse him of hiding weapons or plotting murder? Hadn't my father even urged the desperate Tutsi refugees at our house not to kill Hutus, even if the Hutus were trying to kill them?

Pastor Murinzi told me that he'd gotten his information from the authorities. Unfortunately, like so many other Rwandans, he blindly believed what he was told by people in power.

My spirits plummeted. I felt certain that no one would spread such blatant lies against my father . . . not unless they'd killed him first. Making him out to be a dangerous man was obviously how they planned to justify his murder. But I couldn't think about that. I refused to entertain the idea of anyone in my family being dead—not now. I wasn't strong enough yet.

I was so angry with the pastor that I wanted to scream, but how could I do anything? He was all that stood between us and death. We were completely dependent upon his charity—even if he wasn't being very charitable at the moment. We could tell that he no longer saw us as his neighbors who were in danger and in need of help. Now he viewed us the way the killers did: as nonhumans, cockroaches that were destined to be exterminated before the war was over.

My anger boiled inside me as Pastor Murinzi abused my father's good name. I couldn't control my temper—my father had suffered enough indignities! I raised my voice for the first time since he'd locked us away in the bathroom: "If my father had so many guns, why didn't he pass them out to the thousands of Tutsis who came to us looking for protection? If my father had so many weapons, why didn't he stop the killers when they burned our house to the ground? If he'd planned to kill Hutus, he would have killed them before they drove his family into hiding and destroyed his life! Tell me, Pastor, why didn't he use the guns to protect his wife and daughter from killers and rapists?"

Pastor Murinzi was shocked by my outburst (and so were the ladies—their eyes opened wide in disbelief as they watched me challenge the man who held their lives in his hands). He waved at me to be quiet—then he told me that guns had also been found in the church of Father Clement, the kindly old priest I'd asked to make me a nun when I was a child. Father Clement was the gentlest soul I'd ever met. He was a lifelong vegetarian because he couldn't stand to see an animal hurt; he was also repulsed by violence and hated guns. The pastor's claims were such obvious lies that I had to challenge him.

"Did you see any of these weapons, Pastor?"

"No . . . but I heard about them from important people. They're honest and wouldn't lie."

I couldn't believe that it was possible for an educated man to be so naive, especially with what was happening in the country. "So, you have no proof of the things you accuse my father of?"

He took a blank piece of paper out of his pocket and said that it was the type of paper RPF rebels gave to people who donated guns and money. "It was found at your house," he said, waving it in front of me as if he were holding a smoking gun.

"It's just a blank piece of paper."

"But it's the kind of blank paper that the rebels use."

I couldn't stand talking to him anymore. "Well, if that's the kind of evidence you use to condemn a man, then I can understand why killing comes so easily to people around here."

The pastor stuffed the little piece of paper back into his pocket and turned to leave.

"Wait," I called to him. "Do you have a Bible you could lend me? I forgot mine at home."

He seemed embarrassed—he knew my home was a charred ruin—and agreed to bring me one. I was grateful . . . I needed to cleanse my mind with God's beautiful words.

The other ladies looked at me as though I'd lost my senses. They thought that I'd needlessly, recklessly challenged the pastor's patience and authority. Maybe I had, but I didn't care. I felt obligated to defend my father, and at that moment, the pastor seemed more like a jailer than a savior.

Besides, the fact that Pastor Murinzi felt comfortable speaking ill of Dad was a pretty good indication that he thought our days were numbered. Rwandans are intensely private and secretive people who keep their emotions to themselves—the pastor would never have bared his feelings to me if he thought that I would survive the holocaust and meet him again one day as an equal.

I WAS PRAYING TO RID MYSELF OF MY NEGATIVE ANGER when Pastor Murinzi turned on the radio in his bedroom.

The new president of Rwanda was speaking, and our ears perked up when we heard him say the name of our home province, Kibuye. His voice was exuberant—could it be that the war was over? Would we finally be able to leave the bathroom and go find our families? The six of us looked at each other eagerly, thinking that we were going to hear some good news at last. But our hopes were smashed as we listened in horror.

"I want to personally congratulate the hardworking Hutus of Kibuye for their excellent work," the president said. "More of our Tutsi enemies have been killed in Kibuye than in any other province."

I felt sick. Did the world not see the madness that had seized this country? Was no one going to come and help us?

The president was so pleased with the "good work" being done in Kibuye that he promised to send thousands of dollars to buy food and beer so that the killers could celebrate properly: "After you finish the job and all the enemies are dead, we will live in paradise. We will no longer have to compete for jobs with cockroaches. With no little cockroaches, there will be plenty of space for Hutu children in our schools." It must have been a live broadcast, because we could hear people clapping and cheering.

"You have been doing fine work in Kibuye—almost all our enemies are dead. But we must kill them all. Let's finish the job!"

We looked at each other in despair. Could he really mean that almost *all* the Tutsis in our area were dead? There were more than a quarter million Tutsis in Kibuye . . . how could this be? What about our families? Where were my parents and Vianney and Augustine? Oh, where was my sweet Damascene? I asked God if He was testing me—and once again, I put my hands together to pray. Yet it was difficult to find my quiet place to talk to God while the devil was screaming in my ears.

After the president's broadcast, we heard voices through the window, one of which belonged to my old friend Janet. She was standing in the yard on the other side of the bathroom wall, and she was talking about me. "Immaculée?" she said. "Nobody has found her yet. I thought that she was a friend of mine, but she was a liar. She just pretended to like me to trick me into feeling safe. She knew that her father was planning to kill my family . . . I really don't care if they find her and kill her."

Oh, God, what next? I wondered. *How could Janet say such things?* I knew that she'd been upset when I saw her last, but I figured that it must be her father's influence and the stress of the war. But here she was, my oldest and dearest friend, saying that she didn't care if I lived or died.

Hearing Janet renounce me made me feel so terribly lonely that I desperately needed to talk to a friend. I wished that I were back in my dorm, laughing with Sarah and Clementine, or unburdening my sorrows to them while they held my hands and comforted me.

The devil must have been eavesdropping on my thoughts because no sooner had I heard Janet deny my friendship than another report came across the pastor's radio—this one announced the death of hundreds of students on my campus. It was a massacre.

"We have scorched the earth in Butare . . . we have killed more than 500 snakes and their Hutu traitor friends at the university," the announcer bragged.

It pained me to think of all my university friends, many of whom had been close friends since high school. I knew for certain that a lot of them had stayed on campus over the Easter holiday. I thought about all those lovely girls that I'd laughed with, cried with, and prayed with . . . and all the dreams we shared about growing up, falling in love, and having families. We were sure that we'd be friends for life—now their lives were over, extinguished. I prayed that they hadn't been tortured. Then I realized that I would have been with them if I hadn't received my father's beautiful letter pleading with me to come home for the holidays.

My heart ached. Had I lost *everyone* I'd ever loved? I closed my eyes and prayed for God to show me a sign that He was with me. He was the only One I had left, the One I could trust. But instead of a sign, I heard a cry for help.

"Pastor Murinzi, thank God you're here! Please, you must help me. They're coming for me . . . they're coming to kill me!"

I recognized the woman's voice: It was Sony, an elderly widow whose husband had been murdered in the 1973 killing spree. She was a kind old woman who always greeted me when I got off the bus from school with fruit and little presents for my brothers. She was like a grandma to me, and I wanted to stand up and shout to her to come and hide with us.

But then I heard the pastor say: "Get away from here. I can't hide Tutsis, I'm sorry. You can't come in here."

"Have mercy on me, Pastor, please. You are a man of God—please spare my life . . . I won't tell anyone. I'll be quiet. I don't want to die, Pastor. I'm just an old lady, I've done no one any harm."

"You are an enemy of the country, and I can't shelter you. I am a good Hutu, so leave." And he slammed the front door.

In the distance I could hear the killers singing their hunting song as they approached the house. Poor Sony began to scream again. I could see her in my mind, hobbling away on her cane and bowed legs—she wouldn't get very far before the killers caught up with her.

I wanted to cry, but no tears came. My heart was hardening to the constant onslaught of sorrows. I didn't even feel anger toward the pastor. Perhaps the killers were very close when Sony arrived and he had no choice but to turn her away.

I closed my eyes and asked God to receive Sony's kind soul and make sure that there was a place in heaven for her. Then I once again asked Him for a sign that He was watching over us.

The pastor opened the door and, without saying a word, handed me the Bible I'd asked for earlier.

I opened it immediately and looked down at Psalm 91:

> This I declare, that He alone is my refuge, my place of safety; He is my God, and I am trusting Him. For He rescues you from every trap and protects you from the fatal plague. He will shield you with His wings! They will shelter you. His faithful promises are your armor. Now you don't need to be afraid of the dark any more, nor fear the dangers of the day; nor dread the plagues of darkness, nor disasters in the morning.
>
> Though a thousand fall at my side, though ten thousand are dying around me, the evil will not touch me.

➤◀

CHAPTER 13

A Gathering of Orphans

More than a month passed, and we thought that we'd never see the sky again. The killers came and went as they pleased, arriving unannounced at the pastor's door at all hours of the day or night. It could be a few dozen or a few hundred of them—they came when they were ordered to, when they received a tip, or if they grew bored and wanted to hunt for new Tutsis to torture or kill. But they always came, and we knew that they'd keep on coming until they found us, or until they lost the war.

The news reports on the pastor's radio were bleak: Government leaders had turned every single Rwandan radio station into a propaganda death machine. The announcers told Hutus everywhere that it was their duty to kill Tutsis on sight, no questions asked. And the country was still completely shut down to ensure that work didn't interfere with killing. When some farmers complained that their crops were dying, a government official announced over the radio that if someone had to take a day off from killing to tend to their fields, then they must arm themselves while they worked.

"You must not let your guard down! These Tutsi snakes are hiding in the grass and bushes," he said. "So make sure that you have your machete ready to chop the snakes in half. Better yet, take your gun and shoot them! If you don't have a gun, the government will bring you one. If you're working your field and spot a Tutsi woman in the bushes breast-feeding her baby, don't waste a golden opportunity: Pick up your gun, shoot her, and return to work, knowing that you did your duty. But don't forget to kill the baby—the child of a snake is a snake, so kill it, too!"

The local officials handed out machetes at the village gas station while the militia went door-to-door delivering guns and grenades. In fact, one night when Pastor Murinzi came to give us our food, he sported a rifle slung across his shoulder. "Don't worry, I'm not planning to shoot you," he said, waving the gun in front of him. "Some government soldiers came by today and gave this to me. If I'd refused to take it, they'd have accused me of being a moderate and shot me." He turned the weapon over in his hand before slinging it back over his shoulder, promising, "I won't use it unless absolutely necessary."

It seemed that every Hutu in Rwanda had a gun or machete, along with orders to use them on Tutsis—and no one in the world was lifting a finger to stop them. We knew from radio reports that help was *not* on its way, and I couldn't understand how other countries, especially the so-called civilized ones in the West, could turn their backs on us. They knew that we were being massacred, yet they did nothing.

The UN had even withdrawn its peacekeeping force shortly after the killing began. However, Roméo Dallaire, the Canadian general in charge of the UN peacekeepers, refused to obey his orders to leave and remained with a couple hundred soldiers. He was a brave and moral man, but he was also alone in a sea of killers. We heard him often on the radio begging for someone, *anyone,* to send troops to Rwanda to stop the slaughter, but no one listened to him. Belgium, our country's former colonial ruler, had been the first to pull its soldiers out of the country; meanwhile, the United States wouldn't even acknowledge that the genocide was happening! It was impossible for them not to know that our politicians wouldn't stop the killing until every Tutsi man, woman, and child was dead. Anybody could hear what they planned to do—what they were doing—by tuning in to any radio station.

Sometimes the pastor would tell us details of the official genocide plans that weren't included in the radio broadcasts. "Once the Tutsis are all dead, they're going to make it look like they never existed. They will erase every trace of them," he told us matter-of-factly. "The government officials I know in town have orders to destroy all Tutsi documents. They've already burned most of the school and work records and have moved on to the birth, marriage, and death certificates. It's the same in every town and village: The orders are to make sure that not even a single Tutsi footprint is left on Rwandan soil."

The only good news we heard was about the war. The Hutu government kept reporting that it was killing all the rebel Tutsi soldiers in the RPF, but then we'd hear on the BBC and other foreign stations that in some parts of the country, the RPF was winning the war. Sometimes we'd hear RPF leader Paul Kagame encouraging Tutsis not to lose faith because the rebels were fighting to save them. He was a hero to us, although we knew that the rebels were fighting around Kigali and farther north—a long way from Mataba. Kagame's words didn't change our situation, but they did give us a little hope that Tutsi soldiers might rescue us one day.

AS THE WAR DRAGGED ON, THE PASTOR BECAME INCREASINGLY worried about what he was going to do with us. "If the fighting lasts many months more, I'll run out of food to feed you. It will be impossible for me to keep you," he fretted.

I remembered the gun that had been slung over his shoulder and wondered what he planned to do when the food ran out. I couldn't allow myself to believe that he'd turn into a killer—not after risking his life to save us. But I certainly knew that he was capable of kicking us out of the house in the middle of the night, just as he'd done to Augustine and Vianney. I also knew that the countryside was crawling with killers and that we wouldn't last an hour outside of the bathroom.

The pastor must have thought a lot about it, and finally he decided that he needed God's help. One night he asked us to pray with him that God would help the government soldiers win the war. We just looked at him . . . didn't he realize what he was asking us to do? I couldn't believe how insensitive he'd become to our suffering.

Nevertheless, we were in a tight spot—what else could we do? We all put our hands together and pretended to pray with him. What I actually prayed for were the souls of the thousands and thousands of Tutsis who had already been murdered. Then I prayed for the killers to come into God's powerful light and be changed by His love: *Touch them with Your Divine love, God. Only then will they drop their machetes and fall to their knees. Please, God move them to stop their slaughter. Forgive them.*

I also prayed that the pastor would not grow too callous toward us, that his heart would not harden at the sight of us, and that he would remember that we were human beings.

As soon as we'd finished praying with him, Pastor Murinzi shocked us by revealing what he intended to do with us after the war: "There will be no Tutsis left in Rwanda once the killing is over, so I'll have to smuggle you out of here without anyone seeing. And you'll have to go someplace where no one knows you, where no one can find out that I was the one who hid you during the war."

It turns out that he planned to send us to live on a remote island 50 miles away in the middle of Lake Kivu to become wives of Abashi tribesmen!

We looked at each other in disbelief. The Abashi were a primitive tribe who lived deep in the forest and had virtually no contact with the outside world. They had no schools, churches, or even jobs; they wore no clothes except loincloths; and they ate only what they could forage or hunt in the forest. Rwandan parents scared unruly children into behaving by threatening to send them to live with the Abashi—it was like being sent to live with the bogeyman. Just about the worst thing you could tell a Rwandan lady was that she'd marry an Abashi man.

"What else is left for you? There is nothing to discuss," the pastor said with finality, and left us to ponder our fate.

I HATED THE WAY THE PASTOR HAD COME TO THINK OF US, but I could understand his mind-set. If the Hutu extremists finished what they started, we'd be the last living Tutsis in Rwanda—we'd be orphans in a hostile homeland.

But I didn't feel like an orphan at all. I'd been praying continually for weeks, and my relationship with God was deeper than I'd ever imagined possible. I felt like the daughter of the kindest, most powerful king the world had ever known. I surrendered my thoughts to God every day when I retreated to that special place in my heart to communicate with Him. That place was like a little slice of heaven, where my heart spoke to His holy spirit, and His spirit spoke to my heart. He assured me that while I lived in His spirit, I'd never be abandoned, never be alone, and never be harmed.

I sat stone-still on that dirty floor for hours on end, contemplating the purity of His energy while the force of His love flowed through me like a sacred river, cleansing my soul and easing my mind. Sometimes I felt as though I were floating above my body, cradled in God's mighty palm, safe in His loving hand. In my mind, I heard myself speaking in exotic languages I'd never heard before—I instinctively knew that I was praising God's greatness and love.

During my waking hours I was in constant communication with God, praying and meditating for 15 to 20 hours every day. I even dreamed of Jesus and the Virgin Mary during the few hours I slept.

In the midst of the genocide, I'd found my salvation. I knew that my bond with God would transcend the bathroom, the war, and the holocaust . . . it was a bond I now knew would transcend life itself.

I lifted my heart to the Lord, and He filled it with His love and forgiveness. Being in that bathroom had become a blessing for which I'd be forever thankful. Even if my parents had perished in the bloodshed outside, I would never be an orphan. I'd been born again in the bathroom and was now the loving daughter of God, my Father.

ONLY THE YOUNGEST OF PASTOR MURINZI'S TEN CHILDREN, his son Lechim and daughter Dusenge, had been living with him when we arrived. But as the war progressed, his other kids returned home, and the house began to fill up. It became more difficult for the pastor to watch over us alone—so after five weeks or so of keeping our existence a carefully guarded secret, he unburdened himself to Lechim and Dusenge, the two people he trusted most in the world.

Lechim was a good man with a wonderful heart, and Dusenge was a very kind girl who'd been a dear friend of mine for a long time. I'd overheard them speaking on many occasions and knew that they were truly appalled by what was being done to the Tutsis.

The pastor told us that he was bringing them to see us, and when he opened the door, all I saw in his children's eyes was pity and compassion. Dusenge greeted me kindly, while Lechim took my hand in his and held it tightly. "Oh, Immaculée," he whispered before falling silent. We'd last seen each other on the day I went into hiding, and we couldn't find the words to describe what had happened since. He squeezed my hand and said, "I'm so happy that you're hiding here . . . thank God my family can do something for you. We will keep you safe."

His kindness reminded me of the good feelings of our innocent relationship years ago. I was coming to see that God created no co-incidences—He'd brought Lechim and me together years ago so that now I could be saved while hiding in his house.

Seeing my old friends was a great comfort to me, even though neither had news of my family or the whereabouts of my boyfriend, John. (It was difficult to communicate in the country because phone lines had been down since the beginning of the war.) But Lechim and Dusenge did bring some tenderness to the bathroom, and on occasion, the rare pleasure of a simple cup of tea.

Pastor Murinzi may have written us off as orphans, but his youngest children had adopted us.

LATE ONE NIGHT IN THE MIDDLE OF MAY, the bathroom door flew open. Suddenly, two young Interahamwe killers towered above us. We flinched, expecting a machete blow at any second, but then we heard the pastor's voice whispering that we should sit still and not worry. A moment later we realized that the figures weren't killers at all, but two Tutsi women desperate to join our hidden sorority.

We were happy to see two other living, breathing Tutsis, but we couldn't find a place for them to sit. The pastor shoved them into the room, and they fell on top of us. "Don't make any noise," he reminded us again, and closed the door. The girls' faces were just visible in the dim light seeping through the window. We tried talking to them in our sign language, but of course, they didn't know what we were saying. We risked a few minutes of hushed conversation to find out where they'd come from and what was happening in the outside world.

Their names were Malaba and Solange: Malaba was about my age—I'd seen her a couple of times while growing up but didn't know her well, and Solange was a teenager whom I'd never met before. Unbeknownst to us, Marianne, one of the pastor's elder daughters, had been hiding the two girls at her home in northern Rwanda since the genocide had started. The civil war with the rebels was fiercest in the north, and the Hutu extremists were looking everywhere for Tutsi spies. Marianne had a reputation for being kind and compassionate, which made her highly suspicious in the eyes of the extremists. Her house had been searched several times, and she feared that sooner or later Malaba and Solange would be discovered.

Somehow Marianne managed to obtain a fake identity card for Malaba and disguised both of them in costumes similar to the ones the killers liked to wear. She put the machetes, guns, and hand grenades that the Interahamwe had given her to kill Tutsis into her car and seated the girls beside the weapons. Then, as the fighting raged all around them, they began the long, dangerous drive south to her dad's house, where she hoped they'd all find safety.

Malaba and Solange told us that every few miles, Interahamwe killers would stop them at roadblocks and ask for their identity cards. Because Solange didn't have a card, the women thought that they'd be killed at every stop. Having no identity card was as bad as having a Tutsi one . . . which was a death sentence.

"One man handed them his Tutsi card and they chopped his head off right in front of us," Solange whispered hoarsely, shaking her head, unable to believe what she'd witnessed with her own eyes.

"They even killed Hutus who had forgotten their identity cards at home," Malaba said. "I recognized one of the men they killed—I knew he was a Hutu, but they didn't. He was a little taller than they were . . . that's all it took. They called him a Tutsi spy and shot him. Then they killed another Hutu because he argued with them . . . all he said was that it was wrong for them to be killing Tutsis."

Before they began their journey, Marianne told the girls that they'd better be able to act like killers if they wanted to survive. So every time they were pulled over at a roadblock, they picked up a machete or gun and shook it in the air.

"We screamed like crazy women," Solange said. "We'd shout, 'Hutu Power! Hutu Power! Kill all the cockroaches! Kill those Tutsi dogs!' The killers loved seeing us act like that—they'd tell us to keep up the good work and wave us through. Wanting to kill Tutsis is like having a passport . . . the country has gone mad. And most of those guys were drunk or high on marijuana. In fact, we saw soldiers pull up in Jeeps at two checkpoints and pass out drugs and alcohol to the killers to keep them motivated."

The two sisters told us that they'd passed so many dead bodies on the road heading south that it took them a long time to realize that they were seeing corpses. "There were so many, and they were stacked so high that we thought we were passing by piles of old clothes and garbage. But when we looked closer . . . when we stopped and rolled down the window, we knew. You could hear the buzz of the flies over the sound of the car engine. And there were hundreds of dogs eating the bodies, fighting over body parts . . . it's all so sickening. The whole country reeks of rotting flesh," Solange said. Her face was pale, and she trembled as she spoke. "I can't get those images out of my head . . . even when I close my eyes, all I see are dead bodies."

We would have had a hard time believing what they described if we hadn't already heard similar horror stories on the radio and from the pastor. It sounded like the apocalypse had arrived, and Rwanda was the first stop.

We asked if they had any news of our families, but they didn't even know where their own were. Marianne was Malaba's godmother, which was why they'd been visiting her when the killings began.

Malaba was weeping as she adjusted her position in our laps. "If Marianne hadn't taken us in, we'd be lying in one of those piles of corpses, being eaten by dogs."

The image made me shiver. I wondered for the millionth time where my parents and brothers were and silently asked God to watch out for them: *You're the only family I can talk to now, God. I'm relying on You to take care of the others.*

IT WAS MUCH MORE CROWDED THAN USUAL IN THE BATHROOM THAT NIGHT. As I cradled sweet seven-year-old Sanda in my lap while she fell asleep, I thought about how each one of us in that little room had been torn away from our families, or had had our families torn from us. I stroked Sanda's hair and wished that my own mother could have been there to cradle me.

I drifted off to sleep shortly before dawn and had the most intense dream of my life. I saw Jesus standing in front of me, his arms outstretched as though he were about to embrace me. He was wearing a piece of cloth wrapped about his waist, and his long hair spilled down around his shoulders. I remember being struck by how thin he looked: His ribs protruded, and his cheeks were lean and hollow. Yet his eyes sparkled like stars when he looked at me, and his voice was as soft as a gentle breeze.

"When you leave this room, you will find that almost everyone you know and love is dead and gone," he said. "I am here to tell you not to fear. You will not be alone—I will be with you. I will be your family. Be at peace and trust in me, for I will always be at your side. Don't mourn too long for your family, Immaculée. They are with me now, and they have joy."

I awoke relaxed and happy. Dreaming of Jesus was a beautiful treat, and I relished the warm afterglow, thanking God for sending me such wonderful thoughts. But as the day wore on, my heart became heavy. Jesus had said that my family was dead . . . and I desperately wanted them to be alive. I wanted to see my parents, tell Vianney how sorry I was for letting him go that night, and watch Damascene's smile spread across his face. After all my prayers, why couldn't God spare their lives?

I closed my eyes and comforted myself, thinking that if it were only a dream, my family could very well be alive . . . and if it hadn't been a dream, then God had promised to care for me always, and I'd never known God to break a promise.

NOT LONG AFTER THAT DREAM, I HEARD PEOPLE TALKING outside the bathroom window about some recent killings they'd witnessed. One of the men chose to tell the story of the capture of a young man who'd been hiding in the area since the beginning of the war: "This boy had a master's degree from university, and the killers kept taunting him about it—they asked him why they'd caught him if he was so smart. One of them said he wanted to see the brains of someone with a master's degree, so he chopped the boy across the head with his machete. Then he looked inside the skull."

My heart broke. There were not that many young Tutsi men in the area who'd earned a master's degree . . . I was sure that they were talking about my brother Damascene!

Oh, God, please don't let it be him, I prayed. I tried to calm down, telling myself that I couldn't be certain they were talking about Damascene. I kept praying that it wasn't my brother and waited for Pastor Murinzi to come with our food. When he finally opened the door hours later, I told him what I'd heard and asked him point-blank if the people had been talking about Damascene's murder.

I'd surprised him with my question and noticed that his eyes wouldn't meet mine. "No, no, not at all," he said. "They've been killing many young men, so there's no reason to think that they meant your brother. I haven't heard anything about any of your brothers, Immaculée."

Oh, Pastor, I thought, *I wish you were a better liar!* The expression on his face told me that Damascene was dead . . . but how could I be sure? I bit my lip and thanked him for keeping me informed and for protecting all of us. He nodded and left in a big hurry.

The other women told me not to worry, that my brother was all right, and that there was no way of knowing whom the men had been talking about. I smiled a little, outwardly agreeing with them. After all, there was still a good chance that my beautiful Damascene was alive, and I'd soon see his smiling face again and laugh at his silly jokes.

But my heart wouldn't listen to my head. I began weeping, softly at first, but soon I was sobbing inconsolably. I slapped my face and pinched myself hard all over, hoping that the pain would distract me and stop my tears. But nothing worked. I knew that the other women were panicking, afraid that I'd be overheard, but I couldn't stop myself. I bit my hand to stifle my crying, but the tears kept pouring down my face, and my sobbing grew louder. To make matters worse, the younger girls began crying, too. The older ladies were waving their hands in the air, silently begging me to stop my bawling.

An hour later I did stop. And I never cried in that bathroom again.

>–<

CHAPTER 14

The Gift of Tongues

Seven weeks in the bathroom had left us all frighteningly gaunt—our bones pushed into our flesh, and our skin sagged. Sitting on the hard floor became increasingly uncomfortable as our muscle and fat disappeared, leaving us with no padding on our bottoms. Despite having two additional women with us, the bathroom grew roomier every day. We were shrinking, and our starvation diet left us weak and light-headed much of the time. I could tell by my clothes that I'd lost at least 40 pounds (and I was only about 115 pounds to begin with).

Our skin was pale, our lips were cracked, and our gums were swollen and sore. To make matters worse, since we hadn't showered or changed clothes since we'd arrived, we were plagued by a vicious infestation of body lice. Sometimes the tiny bugs grew so engorged with our blood that we could see them marching across our faces.

We may not have been a pretty sight, but I'd never felt more beautiful. Each day I awoke and thanked God for giving me life, and each morning He made me feel loved and cherished. I knew that He hadn't kept me alive so long and through so much suffering just to let me be killed beneath the machete of a blood-drunk killer! And I knew that He wouldn't let me die from some silly everyday ailment. I was sick twice in the bathroom with illnesses that I could have taken care of in a day with a couple of pills . . . if we'd had any. The first sickness came with a 105-degree fever that left me shaking and delirious. The second was a nasty urinary-tract infection, which was one of the most painful experiences I've ever endured. The only thing the pastor had to offer me was a thermometer and his best wishes—he had no medication to spare.

All I could do was pray, so that's what I did. When the pain and fever became too much to bear, I asked God to lay His healing hands on me while I slept. Both times I awoke refreshed and well, without fever or pain. I'd been cured by the power of His love.

No, illness wasn't going to take me. I was certain that God had a greater purpose for me, and I prayed every day for Him to reveal it to me. At first I was expecting Him to show me my entire future all at once—maybe with a flash of lightning and a clap of thunder thrown in for good measure. But I came to learn that God never shows us something we aren't ready to understand. Instead, He lets us see what we need to see, when we need to see it. He'll wait until our eyes and hearts are open to Him, and then when we're ready, He will plant our feet on the path that's best for us . . . but it's up to us to do the walking.

GOD PUT MY FEET ON THE RIGHT PATH WHILE I WAS LISTENING to Pastor Murinzi talk about the war one day. The pastor was excited because the United Nations was considering sending peacekeeping troops to Rwanda, which he thought might hasten an end to the war. The UN had pulled most of its soldiers out after ten Belgian peacekeepers were murdered by Hutu soldiers on the first day of the genocide. In fact, every Western country had evacuated its citizens from Rwanda when the killing started, leaving the Tutsis to face their fate alone. There had been virtually no outsiders in the country since the genocide began—that had sent a signal to our government that the world didn't care if it were committing genocide, and that the lives of Tutsis didn't matter, so the killing continued.

Even the mere possibility of the UN sending new troops meant a lot . . . it could even stop the genocide! But the pastor said that there was a problem. "The Tutsis in the RPF don't want the UN to send troops because they want to keep the war going. They think they can win the war and take over!" he snorted. "They are so arrogant. They are demanding that if the UN does send troops, they had better be English-speaking troops . . . such nerve!"

The pastor told us that most soldiers in the RPF had grown up in exile in Uganda, which was colonized by Britain, so they spoke English. This contrasted with Rwanda, which had been colonized by Belgium, where French was spoken—so in high school many of us were taught French as a second language.

"The RPF would refuse to speak French, even if they knew how," Pastor Murinzi added. "They claim that the French military trained the Interahamwe killers. They hate the French . . . if the RPF were to win the war, they would probably make us all speak English!"

God turned on a light in my brain.

Actually, it was more like a cannon going off. At that moment, I was absolutely convinced that the RPF would win the war. This meant that I would meet English-speaking people after the genocide and would have to tell them what had happened to us. I also had a pre-monition that I'd be working at the United Nations, where practically everybody spoke English. I suddenly knew with crystal clarity that I would spend the rest of my time in the bathroom learning the English language. I felt as if God had handed me the winning numbers to a big lottery . . . all I had to do was make sure that I was ready when the numbers were drawn. I had to prepare to meet my destiny!

I knew that learning a completely foreign language would re-quire many hours of study, which would force me to cut back on my prayers. I worried that this would give the devil the opportunity he'd been waiting for: to jump back into my head, fill me with fear and doubt, and drag me down into darkness and despair.

I did the only thing I could. I asked God what to do. *Dear God, You put this idea to learn English into my head, so You better help me keep the devil away while I study! Now please show me how I'm supposed to learn a new language while I'm stuck in this bathroom.*

I didn't bother informing the other ladies about my study plans—they already thought I was soft in the head for praying the way I did. If I told them that I intended to master a foreign language while we were fighting for our lives, they might have asked the pastor to pack me off to an Abashi tribesman right away. So I kept my dreams to myself.

The next day when the pastor brought us food, I asked him if he could lend me a French-English dictionary and any other books he might own written in English. He looked at me as though I'd just ordered a steak dinner.

"I only want to occupy my mind a little. We've been staring at the walls for nearly two months, and we can't even talk to each other," I whispered.

He shook his head, turning away as though he were dismissing a lunatic.

"If I learn English, I'll be able to tell the UN peacekeepers after the war how bravely you acted to save our lives," I quickly added.

Pastor Murinzi suddenly warmed up to the idea, promising to look through his collection. I was lucky: Very few Rwandans owned any English books, but the pastor found two, as well as a French-English dictionary.

"But I don't have any English books for beginners, Immaculée. The books I do have would be very difficult for you," he said.

I smiled up at him. I had no way of knowing how long the war would last, but I didn't intend to take baby steps—I wanted to make giant strides toward my new life. "That's okay, Pastor," I responded. "I don't want beginner books because I'm in a hurry. Please bring me the biggest, most difficult English book you have."

The pastor became quite enthusiastic about my plan, even telling me how I'd be able to recognize the UN peacekeepers. "They are the only soldiers who wear blue hats," he said, handing me the two thick English books and the dictionary.

I opened them immediately, feasting my eyes on the exotic-looking words. I held the books like they were pieces of gold—I felt as though I'd been awarded a scholarship to a fancy American university.

I took a deep breath and thanked God for answering my prayers and bringing me the tools I needed to learn English. Even though I'd be losing prayer time, I knew that God would be with me while I studied. He intended for me to learn this language, and I could feel the power of His intention coursing through me. I would not waste a minute of my time in self-pity or doubt. God had presented me with a gift, and my gift in return would be to make the most of His kindness. I opened the biggest book and began to read.

I DEDICATED THE REST OF MY STAY IN THE BATHROOM to praying, meditating on God, and studying as hard as I could. I learned English one word at a time: I'd see a new term in the English book, then use the dictionary to translate it into French and unlock its meaning. It was slow going at first, but it was fascinating . . . and fun!

The first thing I did was memorize the important words I knew I'd need as soon as I was back in the real world. I'd discovered that *I* meant "Je" in French, and realized that it was a very important word for me to remember. I needed to be able to say, "I am Tutsi, I need help," "I have been in hiding for three months," "I am looking for my family," or "I want a job."

At the end of my first day studying English, I'd read the first page of the first book many times. I wish I could remember the name of the work now, or even what it was about, but it's a blur. What I do remember is holding it tightly to my chest when it became too dark to read and silently mouthing my first English sentence: "I am Immaculée." *Thank You, God!*

At the end of each day, I was exhausted but exhilarated. I knew that the new life God had planned for me would reveal itself in this language I couldn't yet understand. As the days passed, I memorized many of the terms I'd need to tell my story in English. *Escape, hiding, war, prayer, job,* and *God* became the cornerstones of my growing English vocabulary—and each new word was as precious as a jewel. I also committed the words *before* and *after* to memory because by then I knew that I'd always refer to my life in terms of before or after the holocaust.

While browsing the dictionary one morning, I discovered a section on English grammar. Rules! I was ecstatic—it was like manna from heaven! I'd found the keys that would unlock the mystery of English: verbs, nouns, and adjectives; conjugation; past, present, and future—it was wonderful! While the other ladies slept or stared into space, I explored a new universe. I said my prayers and read my books all day. I read until well past midnight beneath the faint light from the window, and I read until my eyes refused to stay open. And I thanked God for every second He granted me to study.

Three weeks after I started this endeavor, I'd already read the two books that the pastor had given me from cover to cover. I was ready to move on to the next level: to teach myself to write in English. I borrowed a pen and paper from the pastor and began composing a letter.

I wrote to a man who didn't exist yet, but who was someone I believed in with all my heart—our rescuer. I was so convinced that we'd be rescued that I gave my imaginary hero all sorts of features and characteristics to make our future meeting seem more real. He was a tall, dark-skinned UN soldier with a small moustache and a thick British accent. He wore a clean, freshly pressed blue uniform with a blue beret pulled tightly down toward his right ear. He had a kind, open face; an honest smile; and warm brown eyes that filled with tears of compassion when he read my letter describing our tale of hardship. The image I had of him was exactly the opposite of one I'd formed of the killers.

Writing that letter was an important step for me in developing my new outlook on life. In my mind I painted my rescuer as kind and caring, because that was the kind of person whom I wanted to rescue us. Someone had once told me that it was important to visualize what you want to happen in the future, because doing so could actually help make it come true. Well, thanks to God, I'd become a big believer in that philosophy.

God had planted a seed in my mind. He'd told me to learn English, and that practice was showing me that a rich and exciting life was waiting for me on the other side of the genocide. I knew that whatever I envisioned would come to pass if I had faith and visualized it with a pure heart and good intentions, and if it were something God thought was right for me. It was then that I realized I could dream and visualize my destiny. I vowed that I'd always dare to dream for what I wanted. And I would only dream for beautiful things like love, health, and peace, because that is the kind of beauty God wants for all His children.

In early June, I came face-to-face with my past. My boyfriend, John, and I had been a serious couple for two years, and we'd even talked about getting married after I finished university. Although we'd had a pretty big falling-out before Easter (he'd embarrassed me by calling off an engagement party to formally introduce our families), I still thought that we'd patch things up.

We hadn't been in touch since the killings began, but I thought about him often during my time in the bathroom, praying that he was safe and unhurt. Because he was Hutu, I knew that he was probably out of harm's way and free to move around the countryside as he wanted. Many times I wondered if he was searching for me, trying to find out if I was dead or alive and hiding someplace, waiting for him to come to my rescue. Those questions, and a few others, were answered for me when I least expected it.

Late one morning we heard a big commotion at the front of the house. I automatically assumed that another search party of killers had arrived to hunt for us . . . but I quickly realized that this ruckus was different. We didn't hear vile killing songs or the usual threats, cursing, and shouts of anger—instead, there was happiness in these voices, even joy. Arrivals at the house had always brought fear to my heart, but this time it brought tenderness and warmth. Amid the welcoming sounds of old friends reuniting, I heard John's laughter, and my breath caught in my throat.

It turns out that he'd come down from Kigali with much of Pastor Murinzi's extended family. Like thousands of Hutus, they were fleeing the capital as the rebel Tutsi soldiers pushed closer and closer to the city. Afraid of reprisal killings, they'd abandoned their homes and headed south, where there was no fighting. At least 40 of the pastor's relatives, including John, planned to resettle in our village in the hopes that the war would pass them by.

I was so thrilled to know that my boyfriend was alive, healthy, and even in good spirits—it was exciting to think that we could soon actually see each other. I spent much of the day wondering if he knew that I was hiding in the house.

Very late that night, when everyone else was asleep, the pastor brought John to the bathroom. I was so happy to see him that I actually forgot where I was for a few minutes—and I hugged him so hard that I nearly passed out from the exertion. After weeks of communicating in whispers and sign language, I had trouble finding my voice to tell him how much I'd missed him and had prayed for him.

John stepped back quickly, looking me up and down before finally saying, "I can't believe how skinny you are, Immaculée. Hugging you is like holding a bag of bones!"

I looked at him, laughing and crying at the same time. I was taken aback by his first words to me, though—I was hoping that he might tell me he loved me, or at least say how happy he was to see me alive.

"Well . . . you don't have that great body anymore," he went on, "but you still look good! I've been praying you'd still be alive and that no one had raped you. And here you are, alive and unraped!"

His words made me feel awkward; in fact, it was as if somebody else were saying them, not my boyfriend. He seemed different from when we'd last been together. He certainly *looked* different—he'd grown his hair out in a wild Afro style, and his face was hidden behind a shaggy beard. He explained that he hadn't been able to find a barber because everything in the country was closed down while the genocide was being carried out.

Pastor Murinzi cut off our visit after a few minutes, saying that someone might overhear us. I wished that we could have stayed together longer and talked from the heart, but it wasn't to be. John and I hugged one more time before the pastor closed the bathroom door.

I thanked God for keeping John alive and safe . . . but I soon found his presence in the house disturbing. He was free, living like a prince—walking outside, eating real food, sleeping in a bed with clean sheets, and even talking with his mother—while I was trapped like an animal. Every day I heard him through the bathroom window enjoying himself, laughing, telling stories, and making wisecracks while playing basketball with his Hutu friends. And he *knew* that I could hear him. I didn't expect him to sit around and mope, but carrying on the way he did beneath the window of my bathroom prison seemed highly insensitive. He acted like he was on vacation, while people— my people—were being slaughtered all around him, and his girlfriend was being hunted by thugs and killers.

Sometimes when I listened to him having fun outside, I'd open my Bible and read the following:

> Love is patient and kind; love is not jealous or boastful; it is not arrogant or rude. Love does not insist on its own way; it is not irritable or resentful; it does not rejoice at wrong, but rejoices in the right. Love bears all things, believes all things, hopes all things, endures all things. Love never ends. (1 Cor. 13:4–8)

That was the love I wanted, and I knew it was what God wanted each and every one of us to have.

John saw me once or twice after that first night, and I enjoyed the few minutes we had together. But the visits were too short and infrequent for us to share our thoughts and feelings—and God knows, I had a lot I wanted to share. He didn't seem to make any effort to talk to me, to reach my heart even a little. I knew that it was difficult and dangerous for him to visit, especially with so many of the pastor's Hutu relatives in the house, but still!

I remember pleading with him in one of our brief encounters: "Please, just take the time to write me a little note and send it with the pastor or Dusenge when they bring food at night. That's all I need, John . . . just a few words to know that you're thinking about me, that you still care how I am, and that you want to keep our love alive!"

He promised that he'd write, but he never did. The next time he came to see me, I used a few of our precious moments to chastise him. "Why didn't you write to me like you promised? Do you realize what I'm going through?"

"Well, I know one thing—there are no other men looking at you, and that's one less thing for me to worry about, right?"

With those words, John killed any love left between us. God gave us all the gift of love to share and nurture in one another. It is a precious gift, one that John had squandered.

≫◄

CHAPTER 15

Unlikely Saviors

The first really good news I had in a while came when the killings were at their worst, and evil deeds had become the norm.

In mid-June, more than two months after we went into hiding, I overheard the pastor's son Sembeba talking to some friends beneath the bathroom window. They were discussing recent killings in the neighborhood that they'd witnessed or had been told about firsthand, and the atrocities they described were among the worst I'd heard.

I thought I was going to vomit as one of the boys described unimaginable wickedness as casually as if he were talking about a soccer game: "They grabbed one mama, and all of them took turns with her. She was begging for them to take her children away, but they held her husband and her three little kids with machetes at their throats. They made them all watch while eight or nine of them raped her. When they finished with her, they killed the whole family."

I cradled my head as they swapped horror stories. They talked about children who were deliberately left alive to suffer after their limbs had been chopped off, infants who were dashed against rocks, and HIV-positive soldiers being ordered to rape teenage girls to infect them with their disease.

There was so much more, but I covered my ears and silently pleaded, *Oh, God, if this is what is waiting for us, please take me into Your loving arms now! Let me live in Paradise with You, not in the hell this country has become.*

Eventually the conversation outside turned from the crimes of war to the war itself. Some of the boys said that the government soldiers were getting beaten so badly that Kigali might soon fall to the rebels.

They were all worried about what would happen to the Hutus if the rebels won the war.

Sembeba said he'd heard that France was sending troops to Rwanda. He and his friends all sounded relieved because France had very close ties with the Hutu government. The boys seemed to think that the French would help the government troops fight the rebel Tutsis and drive the RPF out of our country. If that were the case, the war would end, and the killers could complete their evil mission in no time.

At first I wasn't sure how to feel about the arrival of French soldiers. Many people said that France's military helped train the Interahamwe killers, so maybe the troops actually *were* coming to help the government complete the genocide.

But I couldn't believe that would happen. No, if the French came to Rwanda, the rest of the world would be watching them. There would be TV cameras and reporters, which meant that the world would see the killings, the massacres, and the rapes. And if the people in the rich countries saw—*really* saw—what was happening with their own eyes, they'd *have* to do something. They'd have to stop the genocide . . . wouldn't they?

I decided that even if they had helped train the killers, it was a good thing for the French to come, because any foreigner would bring attention to our plight. I prayed for the safe arrival of the troops and thanked God for sending them to us. It was true that, given their history in our country, the French were unlikely saviors. But one thing I'd come to embrace while in the bathroom was that God really did move in mysterious ways.

A few days later we heard a radio report about Operation Turquoise, which was France's plan to send troops to Rwanda. Soldiers from several French-speaking countries would be setting up camp near Lake Kivu, which wasn't that far from us.

Hutu officials threw a big welcoming ceremony at the airport when the troops landed in Goma, which is near the Rwandan border in the neighboring country of Zaire. We listened to the radio as a Hutu choir greeted the soldiers with a song written especially for the occasion. They praised the French and celebrated the long-standing, loving relationship between our two countries.

At my little brother, Vianney's, first communion: I'm on the left at age ten, and Vianney is in the center, with Mom on his right.

My family in front of our home. From left: Dad, Mom, Aimable, Damascene, me, and Vianney.

Here I am with my brothers. From left: Vianney, our friend Claude, me, and Aimable. Damascene is in front.

Here I am at age 17, with Vianney.

Vianney enjoying a day by Lake Kivu.

Sitting behind our house, looking out over Lake Kivu, when I returned to my village after the genocide in late 1994.

Me, wearing the hat, at home with my girlfriend Mimi, who was killed in the genocide. Behind us is my dad's yellow motorcycle.

Me, wearing the striped shirt, picnicking with my Girl Scout friends. My girlfriend Clementine, far right, was killed in the student massacre at our university.

Damascene (holding the ball) was
captain of the basketball team.

Damascene, superstar athlete.

At Damascene's high school graduation: Dad is second from left; Damascene is holding his diploma; I'm fourth from the right; and Vianney is far right, with Aimable next to him.

Here I am at university, a few months before the genocide began.

Damascene visiting me at my university campus in Butare.

Mom, front left, and her best friends. All but one of them were killed in the genocide.

Dad, on the right, discussing Rwandan educational policy at an international conference of Catholic school directors.

Sitting in the bathroom, where I hid with seven other women for three months, during a visit to Pastor Murinzi's house a decade after the genocide.

Wondering how we all managed to fit in that tiny bathroom.

This is the wardrobe that concealed the bathroom door and saved our lives.

Here I am with Pastor Murinzi, ten years after the genocide.

MUHIRWA / D.   6 06 - 05 - 94

. Chers (parents, frère) et sœur,

        Mes salutations filiales et frater-
nelles ! Voilà que nous vivons un cauchemar
sans précédent. Peut-être c'est pour que le
Rwanda soit sauvé. Après un mois sans
nous revoir, je tiens à vous tenir au courant
de la volonté de Dieu: On n'est plus ensemble. Soit
je suis à l'extérieur des frontières du Rwanda, soit
je suis au ciel car je m'y suis préparé. La
certitude est que nous nous reverrons. Les circonstances
sont ainsi. À toi Immaculée Rosa signalera
tout. À mon père et à ma mère aussi. En tout cas
l'extermination d'une ethnie par une autre n'est
possible que si seul Dieu le veut ! Sois
courageuse car il semble que et notre papa, et notre
maman ont été tués. Même Vianney. Vous
je tâcherai de te contacter ! Gros bisous !!

Damascene's heartbreaking letter, written the night before he died.

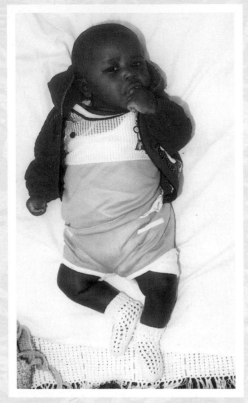

The youngest member of my family to be murdered in the genocide: my eight-month-old cousin, Muvara.

These are fellow survivors, whom I met at the French camp. From left: my cousin Jeannette, her friend Rebeka, my cousin Consolee, Aunt Jeanne, and my cousin Chantal.

The ruins of our family home, destroyed during the genocide.

My brother Aimable stands in the wreckage of Dad's burned-out car.

Me, bottom right, with the soldiers at the French camp.

Judith Garten

Visiting Mother Teresa's Orphanage in Kigali, which became a second home to me after the genocide.

With my wonderful husband, Bryan, during our traditional Rwandan wedding ceremony in Kigali, 1998.

Bryan and me with our babies, our joy: Nikki and Bryan, Jr.

My brother Aimable and I together on his wedding day in 2004.

Here I am chatting with Rwandan president Paul Kagame at the United Nations in New York, September 2005. In 1994, President Kagame led the RPF, the rebel Tutsi army, into Rwanda, and stopped the genocide.

The pastor informed us that the ceremony proved that the French came to Rwanda to kill Tutsis, but I didn't agree. I was sure that God was once again answering my prayers, this time by sending someone to rescue us. The United Nations had thrown its support behind the French plan, which was a good sign. And soon after they arrived, the French themselves announced their intentions on the radio: They said that they were in Rwanda to set up "safe havens" for Tutsi survivors; if Tutsis could reach their camps, the French soldiers would protect them.

"Thank You, God," I whispered.

A few days later a French helicopter started circling our area. We were sure that they were looking for survivors—for *us*—and our hearts soared! From radio reports, I knew that the French were still too far away for us to reach them, and since the war wasn't over, thousands of armed killers still roamed the countryside hunting Tutsis. But it was clear to me what we had to do.

The next time Pastor Murinzi brought us our table scraps, I spoke up. "I think that we should go stay with the French soldiers," I informed him.

"That is a bad idea, Immaculée. You shouldn't believe that they are here to help Tutsis—they would probably kill you as soon as they saw you," he said, dismissing me with a wave of his hand.

"That doesn't matter, Pastor. I would rather be shot quickly by a foreign soldier than give these Interahamwe killers the satisfaction of murdering me. Better to die cleanly at the hands of the French than to die after being abused and degraded by our tormentors."

The pastor seemed shocked by what I'd said, and he told me that the other women and I should all stay in the bathroom and hope for the best. But then he noticed the seven others pointing at me and vigorously nodding their heads in agreement with my suggestion.

"I'd also rather go live in a refugee camp with the French than go to the forest to marry an Abashi tribesman," I added, as the ladies kept nodding their heads. "The French will save us or they will kill us . . . either way, Pastor, I think we'd like to take our chances with them."

He let out a long sigh and shrugged his shoulders—he actually looked relieved by our request. The man had many more people living with him now than at the beginning of the war, and sheltering us was a constant worry for him.

"If going to the French is what you all want, I'll find out where they are and see if it is possible to take you there," he finally consented. "But I wouldn't get your hopes up too high. It is still very dangerous outside . . . a Tutsi seen on the road will be killed instantly."

PASTOR MURINZI WAS WORRIED. He was afraid that three months of confinement in his little bathroom had addled our minds, so he decided that he had to stimulate them. One night while we were waiting for news about the location of the French troops, he came to us with a surprise invitation. For the first time since he'd locked us away, he asked us to join him in the main house for a visit. And not just any visit—he invited us to the movies.

In the wee hours of the night, when everyone else in the house was sound asleep, the pastor led us down the hallway to an empty bedroom where he'd set up a TV and video machine. He shushed us along the way because of the noise we were making. After months of sitting, our legs were wobbly, and we kept bumping into the walls. Nevertheless, I was very grateful to the pastor for giving us a respite from the bathroom, and we were all smiling from ear to ear.

The pastor was worried that we might be overheard, so we watched the video with the volume turned off. Luckily, by that point we'd become expert lip readers and had no trouble understanding the entire movie. I missed the name of the film, but I remember the story vividly. It was about a nurse stationed in a desert village that had no doctors, so to save lives, she was forced to practice medicine without a license. She was persecuted for her good deeds, but was ultimately vindicated—and by the end, she was both triumphant and celebrated.

The story was inspiring, but what I remember most about the movie was a scene where a young boy was singing a song while riding his bicycle through a park. My first reaction was of concern: I was worried that he'd be spotted by the killers and attacked, and I wanted to yell at him to go and hide. Then I remembered that it was only a movie, and it wasn't even set in Rwanda. I'd forgotten that there were places in the world where being born Tutsi wasn't a crime punishable by death. Once I knew that the boy was safe, I desperately wanted to jump through the screen and join him. I wanted to run in the grass, sing a beautiful song, and make a joyful noise unto the Lord! I wanted to live in a world where children laughed and no one was forced to hide.

Unfortunately, the pleasure of our movie night was short-lived. One of the pastor's houseboys had been outside and had seen the blue light of the TV flickering in the window of what he knew should have been an empty room. Hoping for a reward, he reported what he'd seen to a group of killers and told them that he'd long suspected Pastor Murinzi was hiding Tutsis somewhere in the house.

A friend of the pastor warned him that a very large group of killers was preparing to search his home. He told the pastor that they thought he'd been lying to them for weeks and were very angry.

When the pastor came to tell us what had happened, he looked very nervous. I'd never seen him so scared. He dropped onto his knees, and for the first time since we'd arrived, clasped his hands together and prayed for our souls: "Dear God, if it is time for these ladies to go to You, please take them quickly."

I didn't find his prayer at all comforting. He'd frightened us more than we'd ever been—if that was even possible. "Pastor, do you think that the houseboy saw us go back to the bathroom after the movie? Do you really think that they know exactly where we are?" I whispered.

"I'm not sure what they know, but we'll find out soon enough. The killers are on their way. If they know about the bathroom and find you here, they'll kill us all."

>>—<<

CHAPTER 16

Keeping the Faith

I heard the killers call my name.

A jolt of terror shot through me, and then the devil whispered in my ear again: *Now they know who you are . . . now they know where you are. . . .*

My head snapped back, and I was thrown completely off guard. Why did they call out *my* name—how did they know I was here? Were they coming to the bathroom?

I tried to call on God, but all I could hear was the negative voice blaring in my mind . . . along with the vicious, sadistic chants of the killers echoing through the house. Clothes soaked in sweat, I tumbled with my faith.

There were hundreds of them this time. They were yelling at the pastor, accusing and threatening him. "Where is she?" they taunted. "We know she's here somewhere. Find her . . . find Immaculée."

They were in the pastor's bedroom, right on the other side of the wall. Less than an inch of plaster and wood separated us. Their footsteps shook the house, and I could hear their machetes and spears scraping along the walls.

In the chaos, I recognized the voice of a family friend. "I have killed 399 cockroaches," he boasted. "Immaculée will make 400. It's a good number to kill."

As I cowered in the corner, the devil was laughing at me: *They know your name . . . they know you're here. Where is your God now?*

The killers were pressuring the pastor: "Where are the Tutsis? You know what we'll do if we find them. Where is she, Pastor? Where is Immaculée? This is the last place she was seen. Where are you hiding her?"

My spirit tumbled back into the arms of fear and doubt, and I was even more frightened than I'd been the first time the killers came. Their voices clawed at my flesh, and I felt like I was lying on a bed of burning coals. A sweeping wave of pain engulfed my body, and a thousand invisible needles stabbed my flesh. Yet I tried again to pray: *Dear God, forgive me for my lapse of faith . . . I trust in You, God . . . I know that You will save us. You are stronger than the evil in this house.*

The killers were in the room where we'd watched the movie, overturning the furniture and calling out my name again and again. "We want Immaculée . . . it's time to kill Immaculée."

I covered my ears, wishing that I had one of their machetes so that I could cut them off to stop from hearing. "Oh, God . . ." I began to pray out loud, but couldn't form any other words. I tried to swallow, but my throat closed up. I had no saliva, and my mouth was drier than sand.

I closed my eyes and prayed that I'd disappear, but the voices grew louder. I knew that they would show no mercy, and my mind echoed with only one thought: *If they catch me, they will kill me. If they catch me, they will kill me. If they catch me, they will kill me.*

I put the Bible in my mouth and clenched it tightly between my teeth. I wanted to swallow God's words, to gulp them down into my soul. I wanted to find His strength again, but the negative spirit that had haunted me for so long was planting horrid images in my mind. I saw what the killers would do to me when they found us: I saw the torture, the humiliation, the murder. . . .

Oh, God, please! I screamed silently. *Why do You want me to go through this? Why? What else can I do to show You my love? I want to believe that You will save us, God. How can I have more faith? I'm praying so hard, God, so hard . . . but they're so close, and I'm so tired! Oh, God . . . I'm so tired.*

I felt faint—consciousness slipped away from me until the killers' thundering voices were only a soft, distant rumble. Then I was sleeping . . . and dreaming a sweet dream of Jesus.

I floated like a feather above the other women. I saw them trembling below me on the floor, holding their Bibles on their heads, begging God for mercy. I looked up and saw Jesus hovering above me in a pool of golden light, and his arms were reaching toward me. I smiled, and the constant aches and pains that had become part of my body after weeks of crouching disappeared. There was no hunger, no thirst, and no fear—I was so peaceful . . . so happy.

Then Jesus spoke: "Mountains are moved with faith, Immaculée, but if faith were easy, all the mountains would be gone. Trust in me, and know that I will never leave you. Trust in me, and have no more fear. Trust in me, and I will save you. I shall put my cross upon this door, and they will not reach you. Trust in me, and you shall live."

Suddenly I was back on the floor again with the others. Their eyes were still closed, but mine were wide open, staring at a giant cross of brilliant white light stretching from wall to wall in front of the bathroom door. As I looked, radiant energy brushed my face, warming my skin like the sun. I knew instinctively that a kind of Divine force was emanating from the cross, which would repel the killers. I knew that we were protected and safe, so I jumped to my feet, feeling like I had the strength of a lioness. I thanked God for touching me with His love once again, and then I looked down at the others.

For the first and last time while I was in the bathroom, I shouted at my companions: "We're safe! Trust me . . . everything is going to be okay!"

The loudness of my voice hit them like a slap in the face. They looked at me like I was a madwoman, and then they reached up and pulled me down to the floor. I smiled—even though I could no longer see the cross on the door, I knew it was there. The killers had already left the house . . . I heard them singing as they walked away.

The pastor came to see us later that night. "They went straight to where I'd shown you the movie," he explained. "They tore the room apart. When they found nothing, they almost tore the *houseboy* apart. They apologized and left, but it isn't safe here for you anymore. I fired the houseboy . . . now he's angry *and* suspicious. He's friends with the other servants, and I'm sure that they'll all be watching my every move from now on. Let's hope that the French soldiers arrive in our area soon."

For the next week or so, we lived on tenterhooks. The killers visited again, turning Pastor Murinzi's bedroom upside down in their search for any sign that he was hiding Tutsis. And again, they promised to be back.

The pastor was so worried he was being spied on that he cut back on the number of times he'd bring us food. We tried to joke that we'd found a sure way to escape the killers—starving to death—but hunger gnawed at us greatly.

In early July we heard one of the other houseboys knock on the bedroom door. "Pastor, it's been such a long time since I've gotten to the bathroom in there. Why don't I clean it for you now?"

Our spines stiffened . . . would this torture never end?

"Don't worry about the bathroom," the pastor replied. "I've cleaned it myself."

"Oh, you shouldn't do that—that's *my* job. Let me in, and I'll scrub that bathroom good for you."

"No. I've lost the key, so I'm not using the toilet in there . . . now go away. I don't want to be disturbed."

"Maybe I can open it without a key."

"Go away! Didn't I just tell you that I don't want to be disturbed?"

It was the first time in three months that someone had asked to clean the bathroom, so it seemed clear that the houseboy had figured out where we were hiding. We were beside ourselves with worry, certain that he'd go to the killers and tell them exactly where to search: the only room in the house where they *hadn't* already looked!

The pastor came to us after the houseboy left and said that he didn't think he'd go to the killers right away. "They almost killed the last houseboy when they didn't find Tutsis in the place he told them to look," he explained, "so I think this one will wait until he has proof. He might not go to them today, but he will definitely go to them soon."

We looked at each other, knowing that we'd run out of time.

"I heard this morning that the French soldiers are in the area looking for Tutsi survivors—I will talk to them today. Make sure that you're extra quiet while I'm gone," the pastor said, and hurried from the house.

As soon as he left, the houseboy began tormenting us. We could hear him moving around outside the bathroom window all afternoon.

We knew that he was listening for voices or any movement, trying to confirm his suspicions before going to the killers. We didn't move a muscle for hours.

At one point, he dragged a stool or table beneath the window and climbed up. We held our breath as he clambered up the wall, and we nearly fainted when his shadow appeared against the curtain. Thank God the window was just beyond his reach, but he still stood there for the rest of day, waiting and listening. Eventually someone called him away, and we relaxed a bit, although I felt nauseated from the adrenaline that had been pumping through my bloodstream all day.

The pastor returned that evening, but this time he brought good news—maybe the best I've ever received: "I found the French soldiers, and I told them all about you. They're not far away from here, and they said to bring you to them very early tomorrow, between 2 and 3 o'clock in the morning."

We could hardly believe our ears—we were finally going to leave the bathroom! "Thank God," we whispered simultaneously.

But the pastor immediately dampened our spirits. "Yes, thank God," he said. "I just hope it isn't going to be too late for you. After I left the soldiers, I met a friend who told me that the killers are coming back to search my house. They will be here either tonight or tomorrow morning—pray that it is tomorrow."

We prayed very hard.

WE DIDN'T HAVE ANY LUGGAGE TO PACK—all we had were the clothes we'd been wearing every day for three months. Showering was still out of the question, so we contented ourselves with braiding each other's hair. We wanted to be as pretty and presentable as possible for our meeting with the French soldiers. We didn't quite understand that making ourselves look nice was *not* possible at this point.

Pastor Murinzi came at 2 A.M. and told us to wait in his bedroom while he woke his children and told them about us. While we were waiting, we looked at ourselves in his bedroom mirror. It was the first time we'd seen our reflection since we arrived, and the shock almost killed us—we looked like the living dead. Our cheeks had collapsed, and our eyes were set so far back in their sockets that our heads looked like empty skulls. Our rib cages jutted out, and our clothes hung from us as though they'd been draped over a broom handle. I'd weighed 115 pounds when I went into the bathroom; I was 65 pounds when I came out. We all wanted to cry.

When the pastor returned with his ten children, all of them (except Lechim and Dusenge) quickly backed away. They were genuinely shocked and completely confused. The girls began crying; one of them even ran out of the room yelling, "Ghosts! Tutsi ghosts! They've come back from the dead to kill us!" The pastor told her to keep quiet and settle down, and then he explained to them who we were.

None of them could believe that we'd been in the house for so long without them knowing. They touched us—feeling our cheekbones, ribs, and arms—in an attempt to convince themselves that we were really human. They had a hundred questions: "Where have you been? How could you all fit in there? What did you eat? How long have you been here? How could you be so quiet? Did you shower? Didn't you talk? How could you sleep sitting up?"

We tried to answer them, but were exhausted from standing; our muscles and joints were screaming at us for being upright after so many months on the floor.

The pastor told his children to take a good look at us. "There, but for the grace of God, go any one of you," he reminded them. "If you have a chance to help unfortunates like these ladies in times of trouble, make sure you do it—even if it means putting your own life at risk. This is how God wants us to live."

My heart softened toward the pastor. Sure, there had been many times during the past few months I'd been furious with his behavior, and some of the things he'd said were insensitive, ignorant, and cruel . . . but he had risked everything for us, and he had saved our lives. As I stood there waiting to begin the next chapter of my life, I was very thankful. I asked God to watch over this man after we were gone.

All of the pastor's children looked at him with pride, and then looked at us with compassion—all of them except Sembeba, that is. Sembeba was the son we'd overheard weeks before telling his father that Tutsis deserved to be killed, and now he stood in the corner, scowling at the floor. I prayed that one day he would find God's truth and forgiveness, and that he wouldn't tell the killers about us before we got away.

Shimwe, the pastor's daughter who had run out of the room when she first saw us, gave me a towel and one of her own pullovers to wear. She hugged me as hard as she could and told me that she'd pray for me. After so much isolation and depravation, that moment of tender human contact moved me beyond words.

The eight of us said good-bye to the rest of the pastor's children, and then he led us away from the bathroom and into the fresh night air.

≫≪

PART III

A NEW PATH

CHAPTER 17

The Pain of Freedom

The sensations of the night overwhelmed me. The coolness of the air against my skin; the crispness in my lungs; and the brilliant, hypnotic beauty of the billions of stars dancing in my eyes made my soul sing out, "Praise God!"

"What are you staring at? Let's go—we must leave now!" Pastor Murinzi said impatiently as I drank in my first taste of freedom. He was waiting by the gate with the other ladies and John, who wanted to escort us to the French camp. It was a nice gesture, but it came too late. I didn't know if I would survive the genocide—or even live to see the dawn—but I did know that our relationship was dead.

The pastor opened the gate, and his sons (with the exception of Sembeba), burst from the house carrying spears, knives, and clubs. They formed a tight circle around us as we passed through the gate, shielding us from the dangerous eyes of suspicious houseboys and malicious neighbors.

And then we were in the open, walking quickly along the dirt road that had brought me to the bathroom three months earlier. As my eyes adjusted to the darkness, I saw that both Pastor Murinzi and John were armed: John carried a long spear, and the pastor had that rifle of his slung over his shoulder. I wondered what they'd do if we came across a gang of killers. I soon found out.

We didn't see them coming—they appeared out of the night, coming over a small rise in the road. Perhaps 60 Interahamwe were marching in a double line, and while they weren't wearing their frightening uniforms, it was still a terrifying sight. They were heavily armed and moving fast, coming toward us carrying machetes, guns,

139

grenades, spears, and long butcher knives—one of them even had a bow and arrow.

We passed by them so closely that I could smell their body odor and the alcohol on their breath. Remarkably, I was less afraid walking next to them than I'd been hiding from them in the bathroom. Still, I called on God to keep us safe and quell my fear.

The ladies and I stayed in the center of our group escort with our heads down, hoping that the Interahamwe wouldn't notice that we were women. We passed without incident—a few of the killers even said hello and wished John and the pastor good luck as they went by. Either they assumed that we were fellow killers on a late-night hunt, or God had blinded them . . . I thought it was likely both. Besides, at this point in the genocide they wouldn't have expected, or believed, that so many Tutsis could still be alive in one place. They had good reason to think that way, since there were dead bodies everywhere along the road.

God had answered my prayer and had taken away my fear of the killers, but apparently He hadn't extended the same blessing to John and Pastor Murinzi. Both were visibly shaken by our encounter with the Interahamwe. As soon as they were out of view, John and the pastor reassessed their situation.

"You ladies will have to go on from here on your own," the pastor said. "The French are close by . . . go ahead, we'll watch until you're out of sight."

I shook the pastor's hand quickly, and then he, his sons, and John hurried from the road to hide in the bushes. The other women and I were now completely exposed and had no time to waste. The French camp was about 500 yards away, and we ran as fast as our weak legs would carry us.

My heart was pounding when we reached the camp, which was set up on the grounds of an abandoned Protestant nunnery. The rest of the group huddled in front of the gate, looking very frightened, while I rattled it and called out as loudly as I could, "Please help us! Please, we need help!"

It had been so long since I'd spoken above a whisper that my throat ached from trying to shout. My voice was hoarse, and so low that it was nearly inaudible. The ladies panicked when we saw no one waiting to save us, and they started to wail. A few seconds later, six or seven soldiers appeared on the other side of the fence with their machine guns trained on us. I shushed my companions, and because I was the only one who spoke French, told the soldiers who we were and where we'd come from.

The soldiers looked at us skeptically, and their guns were raised and ready.

"It's true! Everything I told you is true . . . we've been waiting for you to save us," I said desperately.

The smallest soldier in the group—a grim-looking, light-skinned man with a shaved head—came to the gate and shone a flashlight in our faces. It was obvious that he was inspecting the shape of our noses. The old myth was that Hutus had flat, broad noses and Tutsi noses were long and narrow. Apparently we passed the test because he opened the gate and let us in. However, he didn't lower his gun while asking to see our identity cards.

I could hear the ladies' breathing quicken—none of them had their identity cards, and they thought that the French were going to shoot them on the spot. Luckily, I'd put mine in my back pocket when I left home three months earlier. The soldier examined my card, which had the word *Tutsi* stamped across it, and then nodded in approval. I immediately vouched for the other women and told them, "I think we're going to be okay."

An emotional dam burst in us as months of pent-up fear, frustration, and anxiety flooded from our souls, and a few of the ladies began to sob uncontrollably. The demeanor of the soldiers changed immediately—they lowered their weapons and spoke gently, their voices filled with kindness and concern. We were given water and cheese, the first palatable food we'd seen in months. We ate greedily, realizing that the French were not going to kill us, as the pastor had predicted.

"It's all right, ladies, it's all right," the small soldier said. "You don't have to worry anymore . . . your nightmare is over. We won't let anyone hurt you. Do you understand? You're safe now; we're going to take care of you."

I translated for the others, and soon we were all crying. It seemed impossible that it was over, but here we were, surrounded by trained soldiers with big guns who were promising not to let the killers get near us ever again.

When we settled down, our rescuers explained that we were in a field encampment and that they'd radio for a truck to transfer us to their base camp ten miles away. They told us that we should get some sleep while we waited.

I wandered away from the others, feeling a desperate need for something I'd been missing for so long—a moment of privacy. I lay down on the ground, absorbing everything around me: the rocks digging into my back, the damp earth in my fingers, the dried leaves scratching my cheek, and the sounds of animals scurrying through the darkness. I was alive, and it felt wonderful.

Staring into the night sky, I was again transfixed by the breathtaking beauty of the milky illumination cast by God's countless stars. The starlight was so intense that I could easily see the road we'd arrived on, the same one that led to my home—that is, if I still had a home. I wondered if my family was safe and hiding somewhere nearby . . . or if they'd crossed over to the next life and now existed somewhere on the other side of the eternal galaxies above me.

My gaze returned to the road. I thought about how my brothers and I had followed it wherever we went. Whether it was to Lake Kivu for the morning swims of our childhood, to school every morning, to church on Sundays, to visit friends and family, or to head off on some wonderful adventure during summer vacations, that road had taken me everywhere I loved. It had run through my life, but that life was gone. The road existed now only as a highway for killers and rapists. I was filled with a deep sadness as it slowly dawned on me that, no matter what happened in the hours and days ahead, things would never be the same.

I closed my eyes and told God that it was up to Him to find me a new road to travel.

I SHIVERED. THE COOL AIR BROUGHT GOOSE BUMPS to my skin, reminding me that I was no longer in the cramped, humid bathroom. I stood up, stretched toward the sky, and then walked about the camp. I was completely unafraid, even when I stumbled across two men sitting in the shadows.

I startled them, and one jumped to his feet. After a second, he cried, "Immaculée, is it you?"

"Jean Paul?"

"How is it you're alive?"

"God has spared me. How is it *you* are alive?"

"God has spared *me.*"

"It's good to see you!"

"It's good to see *you!*"

I wanted to laugh and cry at the ridiculous course of our conversation, and at how wonderful it was to be talking out loud to a friend again. Jean Paul was a good pal of my brothers'.

"Hello, Jean Baptiste, I'm glad so see you, too," I said to Jean Paul's brother, who was still sitting down. Jean Baptiste didn't respond—and I could see why when I knelt down to shake his hand. There was a ragged, inch-wide scar across his neck that disappeared beneath his shirt. It hadn't healed completely, so it was an angry, whitish-red color that stood out in painful contrast to his dark skin. He also had deep cuts on his head, one of which was so deep that I wondered how he'd managed to survive the blow.

"He's not saying much right now . . . too sad," Jean Paul said quietly.

Although Jean Paul himself was extremely sorrowful, we sat down and exchanged stories. I told him where I'd been and described my time at the pastor's. And he told me that the genocide had died down a bit in the north since Kigali had fallen, but it was still very bad in Kibuye province, where we were.

"Kigali has fallen?" I asked, shocked and delighted.

"Yes, but there's still plenty of killing," he replied. "In fact, around here it's even worse than before. The worse the war goes for them, the more vicious they become. They're getting frustrated, too—they've slaughtered so many Tutsis already that they're having a hard time finding more of us to murder."

I was surprised to see that Jean Paul and his brother were at this camp because I'd always thought they were Hutu. They were very dark-skinned; fairly short; and had flat, broad noses—the typical European idea of what a Hutu should look like. It didn't make much sense anymore, as generations of intermarriage had made that concept archaic and deeply prejudicial. But Jean Paul explained that their Hutu looks were part of the reason they were able to stay alive. "That . . . and the kindness of a murderer," he said, before sharing what had happened to his family.

"The killers came a week after the president's plane was shot down. I was visiting my friend Laurent, a Hutu who lived a few houses away, when I heard them arrive at my parents' home. I saw about 300 killers—mostly neighbors and old family friends. They broke through the front door and chopped up everybody: all my brothers, my four sisters, my mom, and my dad. They killed everyone . . . at least they thought they had. Jean Baptiste was still alive, but he was bleeding to death.

"I dragged him for miles through the bushes to a hospital where the doctors wouldn't know us. Then Laurent hid us until the French arrived, but it was awful. He saved us by hiding us, but it was agony to be alive. Laurent would wake us to say good morning every day, then go out and spend hours hunting Tutsis with the people who killed my family. When he'd come back in the evening and make supper, I'd see flecks of blood on his hands and clothes, which he just couldn't wash off. Our lives were in his hands, so we couldn't say anything. I don't understand how people can do good and evil at the same time."

"The genocide is happening in people's hearts, Jean Paul," I said. "The killers are good people, but right now evil has a hold on their hearts."

I told Jean Paul that I would pray for his family. Then I realized that he probably knew what had happened to my parents and brothers, since he'd been in the area throughout the genocide. The question was: Did I *want* to know what had happened to them? Was I strong enough to take it? If I knew for certain that they were dead, there would be no going back to my old self, my old life.

I decided that it was better to face the truth. I'd have to pretend that I already knew my family was dead, otherwise Jean Paul would try to spare my feelings and tell me nothing. I'd have to trick him into telling me what I needed to know. I reached into my pocket for my father's red and white rosary and asked God to give me strength.

"So, Jean Paul, about my father . . . I know they killed him, I just don't know where. I was wondering if you might know any details."

"Oh yeah, I know everything. Laurent was there and saw it all. They killed your father in Kibuye town."

His words pierced my heart like a spear. I pushed my fists into my eyes and turned my face to hide my tears.

"Your dad was killed a day or two after my parents were murdered," Jean Paul went on. "I think it was on April 14th. He'd gone to the government office to ask the prefect to send food to the stadium because there were thousands of refugees there who hadn't eaten for days. That was a big mistake."

Oh, Daddy! Why did you have to be so sweet . . . and how could you have been so stupid? The prefect of Kibuye was like the governor, and he'd been close to my father. But other extremist Hutus who were Dad's friends had betrayed him, so I couldn't understand why he continued to trust them. But I knew that he would have sacrificed his life trying to feed starving people—for him, there would have been no other choice. My eyes were burning and my stomach ached as Jean Paul continued.

"Laurent told me that the prefect called your father a fool and had his soldiers drag him outside. They shot him on the steps of the government office and left his body in the street."

"I see . . . thanks for telling me all this, Jean Paul. It helps," I said, using all my energy to steady my voice. I thanked God for the darkness hiding my face. "And what about my mom? I know she was killed, too, but I don't know how   "

"Oh, Rose?" he broke in. "She was one of the first in the area to die. She was murdered a few days before your father. I think Laurent may have been one of the killers because he knew all the details. Anyway, she was hiding in the yard of your grandmother's neighbor. Someone was being killed nearby, and your mom heard the screaming and thought that it was your brother. She went running into the road shouting, 'Don't kill my child! Don't kill my Damascene!'

"It wasn't Damascene, but as soon as the killers saw your mom, they went after her. They told her that if she gave them money, they'd leave her alone. She agreed and went to borrow some from her friend Murenge. But Murenge ordered her to leave her alone: 'Get away from my house—we don't help cockroaches here!' Murenge told the killers to take your mother into the street to kill her because she didn't want them messing up her yard. They dragged your poor mom to the side of the road and chopped her to death. Some neighbors buried her, though. She was one of the few who got buried . . . soon there were too many bodies and no one left to dig graves."

Every word he told me was torture, but I was a prisoner to the information. I pushed him to tell me more. "Did you happen to hear about my little brother, Vianney?" I asked, feeling a stab of guilt as I remembered how I'd sent my baby brother away from the pastor's house in the middle of the night.

"Vianney was killed at the Kibuye stadium with his friend Augustine. There were thousands of people there—and they were all annihilated. First the killers shot them with machine guns, and then they threw grenades at them. I don't think anybody survived."

My hands were shaking, and I was having a hard time getting air into my lungs. I calmed myself as best I could and tried to ask about Damascene, but I couldn't bring myself to say his name. I clung to the hope that he was alive and waiting for me somewhere. Finally, I said, "My brother Aimable is in Senegal and doesn't know any of this . . . I don't even have an address where I could send him a letter . . . "

"You should ask Damascene's friend Bonn. I know he has all of Damascene's papers and things . . . or at least he used to."

"Why is that?" I asked, my heart racing.

"Oh, because he was hiding your brother, and when Damascene left to go to Zaire, he left all his stuff with Bonn. But he might have gotten rid of his things by now—I heard he went mad after your brother was killed."

The words struck me like a bullet. *Please . . . no . . . not Damascene, too!*

I didn't want to know any more. I stood up, staggered a few feet away, and collapsed. I pressed my face into the earth—I wanted to lie on the cold, cold ground and sleep with the rest of my family. I wanted to hear nothing, see nothing, feel nothing. I had so many tears to cry, and I sobbed into the dirt. Jean Paul was at my side, trying to comfort me. He wiped the dirt from my face and gently rubbed my neck, but I pushed his hand away.

"Please let me deal with this. I have to learn to be on my own now, Jean Paul. No one in this world can comfort me now . . . leave me alone for a while." He walked away to the other side of the camp, taking his silent brother with him.

I lay on my back, looked at heaven, and cried. I cried until I had no more tears. I thought about what Jesus had promised me in my dream and began talking to him. "You told me they would all be dead when I left the bathroom, and you were right," I said. "They *are* all dead. Everything I loved in this world has been taken away. I'm putting my life in your hands, Jesus . . . keep your promise and take care of me. I will keep *my* promise—I will be your faithful daughter."

I closed my eyes and pictured the faces of my family, and I prayed that God would keep them close and warm.

THE METALLIC WHINING OF A TRUCK'S GRINDING GEARS STARTLED ME. A couple hours before dawn, twin beams of light cut through the camp, illuminating the other ladies in an incandescent halo as they stood by the gate with Jean Paul and Jean Baptiste.

The truck sputtered to a stop by the fence. It was a big military transport truck covered with a camouflage-colored canvas tarpaulin. The French soldiers told us to climb in the back and keep quiet.

"There are Hutu roadblocks everywhere," one of them warned.

We reached the first block about a mile from camp, and I could hear the killers' voices on the other side of the canvas. It was all too familiar, except this time we had armed bodyguards. Even so, there were a couple hundred killers and only a handful of soldiers.

"What do you have in the back of the truck?" one of the killers asked.

"We're delivering food and clean water to the Hutu refugees coming down from Kigali," the driver replied.

"Good man! Those Tutsi snakes are killing us in Kigali . . . you can pass, go ahead."

The driver shifted gears, and the truck lurched ahead—we were on our way again. I admired the clever answer the driver had given to get us through the roadblock. Tens of thousands of Hutus from Kigali were running south since the capital had fallen to the Tutsi rebels. Unfortunately, most of the refugees were coming to our province of Kibuye, either to resettle or to try to get to Lake Kivu so that they could cross to Zaire. There were many scared Hutu families trying to escape the fighting, but there were also plenty of new Interahamwe killers in the area as well.

At the next roadblock, the killers waved us through right away. "The French are our people . . . go ahead, let them go!" said one of them. It was the same at the next five roadblocks.

The truck rolled through the night and toward a new day—I wished that it would keep right on rolling into a new *country*. My soul wanted to fly away from Rwanda to another world. I believed that God was planning a new life for me; I just didn't know when or where it would begin. When the truck reached the base camp 30 minutes later, I was keenly disappointed—yes, we were free, but we were still in the middle of Rwanda, still in the middle of the horror.

THE FIRST THING I SAW WHEN I CLIMBED DOWN FROM THE TRUCK was a dilapidated schoolhouse. I noticed that the wooden sign tacked above the door had the word *Rwimpili* scrawled across it, and I realized that we'd come to the school where my mother had her first teaching job.

Sorrow welled up in me, and I had to step away from the others and have a quick talk with God: "Lord, I don't know why You brought me here. I know I will have to mourn my family, but right now I can't . . . please give me the strength I need to survive, and I'll grieve later."

A few minutes later I felt strong enough to walk into the schoolhouse and smile. I remembered my mom's fondness for the run-down, one-room, dirt-floored classroom. "The important thing is what we learn at this school, not the way it looks," she'd say.

Dawn was breaking, and the morning sun filled the schoolhouse, giving me my first look at my fellow survivors. There were about 20 other Tutsis milling about, and suddenly I could see how blessed the ladies and I had been to have stayed in the pastor's bathroom. The other refugees looked far worse off than we did: The poor souls had been living in the open forest for the past three months, sleeping in holes and eating nothing but leaves and grass.

The sun became so bright that I had to shield my eyes, and in the shadow of my fingers, I saw a familiar face. "Esperance!" I cried out. It was my mom's sister, but she didn't seem to hear me.

"Esperance! Don't you know me? It's Immaculée! Thank God someone survived!" I said, hugging her tightly.

She returned my embrace with a feeble squeeze, staring at me vacantly for a long while before speaking. I was worried that perhaps her mind had gone. "It's okay," she said weakly. "I'm happy you're alive. Come see your other aunt." She shuffled listlessly across the schoolyard to where her sister Jeanne and three of my female cousins, all young teenagers, were sitting on the ground.

I stopped about ten yards away and looked at the wretched scene in front of me in disbelief: Their faces were swollen from insect bites; their lips were cracked and bleeding; and their bodies were covered with open sores, blisters, and cuts that must have been infected for weeks. I could smell the sickness from where I stood.

Aunt Jeanne, a teacher, had been a fastidious dresser, and so obsessed with cleanliness that she used to insist that visitors at her house wash their hands before greeting her children. Now she sat in the dirt with her kids, like a group of primitives, their clothing so threadbare I could see their buttocks hanging out.

I dropped to my knees and tried to hug Jeanne, but she avoided my touch and tried to hide her tears from me. "Oh, Immaculée, forgive me . . . I must look a fright. I have something in my eyes that's making them water."

I smiled, thinking that that's exactly what my mother would have said in the same situation, embarrassed by her tears. "Jeanne, I'm so happy to see you." I gently hugged her, then embraced each of the girls. The light slowly returned in their eyes, and tentative smiles crept across their faces.

I said a silent prayer for all of them, asking God to heal their hearts, and promised myself that I'd do everything I could to heal their bodies.

I sat down with them and we began a sad conversation, telling each other who in our family had been killed, and what each of us had been through. Jeanne lost three sons and her husband, while almost all of Esperance's family had been killed. My wonderful grandparents had been murdered, and so had at least seven of my uncles. Soon we were all crying . . . I wondered if our tears would ever stop.

After we'd talked for an hour or so, Esperance handed me a letter. I had no idea how she'd managed to keep it safe and intact all those weeks in the forest. "Damascene found me while I was hiding and gave me this letter for you," she said. "He was on his way to Zaire . . . but he didn't make it."

I took the letter from her hand and looked at the envelope, which was stained with teardrops. I turned and ran from my aunts and cousins—I couldn't bear to be near anyone. Just hearing my brother's name was enough to overwhelm me, and now I was holding the last words he had ever written me. Reading them would be like hearing him speak to me one last time.

≫≪

CHAPTER 18

A Letter from Damascene

I stood alone behind the school and opened Damascene's letter. My heart ached as soon as I saw his quirky handwriting, remembering all the letters he'd written me during the years we were in school—letters that were never sentimental, but always filled with love and tenderness, encouragement and praise, sound advice and gentle chastisements, gossip and humor . . . so much humor. I sat down with my back against the schoolhouse wall and began to read.

> *May 6, 1994*
> *Dear [Dad, Mom, Vianney, and] Immaculée,*
> *It has been nearly a month since we were separated, and we are all living a nightmare. Despite what the circumstances suggest, I believe that a tribe can exterminate another tribe only if it's God's will; maybe our lives are the price that must be paid for Rwanda's salvation. I am only certain about one thing: We will meet again—there is no doubt in my mind.*
> *I'm going to try to get out of the country, but I don't know if I'll make it. If they kill me along the way, you shouldn't worry about me; I have prayed enough . . . I am prepared for death. If I do manage to make it out of Rwanda, I will contact you all as soon as the peace returns. Bonn will tell you everything that has happened to me. . . .*

Damascene's friend Bonn later told me that at this point in writing the letter, Damascene put down his pen, looked up at him, and said, "Bonn, I know that you're my friend and have tried to spare my feelings, but now's the time to tell me—has anyone in my family been killed?"

Bonn was Hutu, so he could travel freely during the genocide and find out which Tutsis had been murdered in the area. He'd kept my parents' and Vianney's death to himself because he'd cared for my brother so much and wanted to protect his feelings.

But when Damascene asked him directly, Bonn told him what he knew. He couldn't bring himself to let Damascene finish writing the letter while believing everyone he loved was still alive. So Bonn told his friend that our dad, mom, and younger brother had been killed, and that I was the only one who might possibly be alive. Damascene cried for most of the day, which explains the teardrops that became a permanent part of his letter.

Before Damascene left to try to catch a boat across Lake Kivu, he took the letter out again and placed brackets around the words *Dad, Mom,* and *Vianney,* and added these lines:

> *Immaculée, I beg you to be strong. I've just heard that Mom, Dad, and Vianney have been killed. I will be in contact with you as soon as possible.*
> *Big hugs and kisses!*
> *Your brother, who loves you very much!*

It was the most painful thing I'd ever read. I ran my fingertips across the tear-stained words and knew that I'd never be able to read this letter without crying.

I DISCOVERED LATER THAT BONN, who will forever be a hero to me, tried to hide my brother in his house against his family's wishes. He succeeded in keeping Damascene safe during the first days of the genocide by secretly stowing him beneath his bed. But when Bonn's family found out what he was doing, they pressured him to turn Damascene over to the killers.

Unfortunately, one of Bonn's uncles was Buhoro, my old teacher who loved to humiliate Tutsi children during ethnic roll call. Buhoro turned out to be one of the most rabid Hutu extremists in the country, and a vicious and prolific murderer—and when he became suspicious,

Bonn knew that he absolutely had to get Damascene out of the house. Late one night he dug a pit at the far end of the family's property and covered it up with wood and leaves. He got Damascene safely out of his bedroom and hid him in the hole only hours before the killers—who'd been tipped off by Buhoro—showed up to search the house.

At Buhoro's insistence, the killers repeatedly searched Bonn's house while Damascene hid in the hole for more than three weeks. But the killers were relentless—they monitored Bonn's activities and eventually spotted him carrying food outside. Worried that they'd search the yard, Bonn and Damascene decided that my brother should head across Lake Kivu to Zaire. (Bonn knew a Hutu Good Samaritan, a fisherman who was using his boat to smuggle Tutsi refugees across the lake to safety.) He pulled Damascene out of the hole after midnight and they made their way to the lake, staying in the shadows, moving from bush to bush. But the journey took too long and they missed that night's boat.

It was almost dawn, and Damascene didn't want to risk the long hike back to Bonn's house, so he stayed with Nsenge, a very good friend of his and Bonn's who lived near the lake. Nsenge was a moderate Hutu who loved our family—my dad had even helped to pay school tuition for several of his brothers—so he was happy to hide Damascene for the day.

Nsenge's brother Simoni was not as generous, however. He welcomed Damascene when he arrived at the house with smiles and friendship . . . but the next afternoon, while my brother slept and Nsenge was out arranging his boat passage, Simoni snuck out of the house, located a group of killers, and betrayed Damascene.

Before supper, Simoni woke my brother and offered to wash his clothes before he left for Zaire. Damascene stripped down to his underwear, and Simoni took his clothes (he later confessed that he'd wanted my brother to feel ashamed and humiliated before he died). After he'd taken the clothes, Simoni called Damascene into the living room, where dozens of killers were waiting for him. They fell on my brother, beating him mercilessly as they dragged him into the street. He was wearing nothing but his underpants.

One of the women who used to work at our house witnessed the whole thing and told me all the details of Damascene's final hour.

"Where is your pretty sister?" the killers had asked my brother. "Where is Immaculée? We've seen the bodies of the other cockroaches in your family, but we haven't had our fun with her yet . . . where is she? Tell us and we'll let you go; don't tell us and we will spend all night killing you. Tell us where Immaculée is and you can walk away."

Damascene looked at them through his broken, swollen face, and—as he had throughout my entire life—stood up for me: "Even if I knew where my beautiful sister was, I wouldn't tell you. You will never find Immaculée . . . she's smarter than all of you put together."

They beat him with the handles of their machetes, taunting him: "Is she as smart as you? You have a master's degree and we caught you, didn't we? Now tell us where your sister is hiding!"

Damascene managed to get to his feet one more time, and then he smiled at the killers. His fearlessness confused them—they'd murdered many Tutsis and always enjoyed listening to their victims plead for their lives. Damascene's composure robbed them of that pleasure.

Instead of negotiating or begging for mercy, he challenged them to kill him. "Go ahead," he said. "What are you waiting for? Today is my day to go to God. I can feel Him all around us. He is watching, waiting to take me home. Go ahead—finish your work and send me to paradise. I pity you for killing people like it's some kind of child's game. Murder is no game: If you offend God, you will pay for your fun. The blood of the innocent people you cut down will follow you to your reckoning. But I am praying for you . . . I pray that you see the evil you're doing and ask for God's forgiveness before it's too late."

These were my brother's last words. Although nothing will ever take away the pain of his brutal murder, I'm proud that he stood up to his killers and died with the same dignity that he lived with.

One of Simoni's brothers, a Protestant pastor named Karera, scoffed at Damascene's speech. "Does this boy think that he's a preacher? *I* am the pastor around here, and I bless this killing. I bless you for ridding this country of another cockroach." Then he looked at the killers and said, "What are you waiting for? Are you cowards? A cockroach is begging you to kill him—why do you stand there? *Kill him!*"

Karera shamed the killers into committing murder.

"You Tutsis have always acted so superior to us Hutus," one of the young killers shouted in Damascene's face as he raised his machete. "You think that you're so much smarter than we are with your master's degree? Well, I want to see what the brain of someone with a master's degree looks like!"

He swung his blade down into my brother's head, and he fell to his knees. Another killer stepped forward and, with a double swing of his machete, chopped off both of his arms. The first killer took another turn with his machete, this time slicing Damascene's skull open and peering inside. Covered in my brother's blood, he began prancing around the neighborhood, bragging that he'd seen a master's degree inside someone's brain.

I never allow myself to dwell on the details of Damascene's murder. I think only of how he faced death, how he smiled before he died, and how he prayed for those who killed him. He was my heart, my brave brother, my sweet Damascene. . . .

Later I heard that one of the killers (a young man named Semahe, who had been schoolmates with Damascene) broke down and cried for days after the murder. He talked incessantly about all the things he and Damascene had done together, such as playing soccer, singing in the choir, and being altar boys. He was haunted by the kindness my brother had shown him and all the other boys they'd known. Semahe expressed his remorse to anyone who would listen.

"I will never kill again," he said. "I will never get Damascene's face out of my head. His words will burn in my heart forever. It was a sin to kill such a boy—it was a sin."

>><<

CHAPTER 19

Camp Comfort

The French camp was an armed fort that kept Tutsis in and Hutus out. The soldiers parked eight tank-like armored vehicles in a semi-circle in front of the school buildings, and the outer perimeter of the camp was patrolled day and night by at least 100 guards. We stayed inside the semicircle of armored vehicles with 30 soldiers who were assigned to protect us around the clock, and to escort us into the forest whenever nature called.

The French soldiers continually apologized for the deplorable conditions we were forced to live under, which made me laugh. Compared to where we'd come from, we were living a life of total comfort. For starters, we could fetch water from a stream and wash ourselves and our clothes with soap!

We slept outside, which the French also thought was a major hardship, but I welcomed it. Even though I often woke up covered in dirt and twigs and aching from lying on rocks and stones, I loved falling asleep staring at the stars—it was like seeing the face of God at the end of the day.

We weren't allowed to cook, which didn't really matter because there was no fresh food. The soldiers fed us packaged cheese and crackers, tins of powdered milk, and canned fruit. It was a limited diet, but I slowly began filling out a bit and stopped adding notches to my belt.

The French said that their job was to protect us, and they did it well—I never once felt threatened by the killers while I was at the camp. However, Hutus did often gather along the outer perimeter, peering between the armored cars to catch a glimpse of us. They stared at us like we were zoo animals . . . sole survivors of a species hunted to the brink of extinction.

"They look at you like you're animals, but *they* are the animals," the captain of the troops said to me one morning shortly after my arrival. When he learned that I was fluent in French, we had a long conversation. I told him my story, and he seemed very sympathetic. He knew what Tutsis had been through in Rwanda and about our history and ethnic conflicts.

"Between you and me, I don't know how the president of my country can live with himself," he said. "France has blood on its hands, since we trained a lot of these Hutus how to kill."

This was the first time I'd heard a foreigner accept blame for what had happened in Rwanda, and it did my soul good. I often despaired listening to the pastor's radio, realizing that the world knew what was happening to us but chose to ignore it.

"Thank you for being so understanding," I replied. "The people who are doing this are very bad."

"Bad? *Bad!* Immaculée, they're evil. They're monsters! I want you to know that you're safe. As long as I'm in charge here, no harm will come to you," he said, patting the gun holstered on his hip. "I'll do more than protect you—I'll give you some justice. Again, this is just between you and me, but if you want revenge, it's yours for the asking. Give me the names of the Hutus who were searching for you, or the ones who killed your parents and brothers, and I'll have them killed for you."

His offer shocked me. It's what I'd wished for during my early days in the bathroom, when the pastor told us about the atrocities being committed against us. I'd wished for weapons—for guns and cannons to kill the Hutus—because I wanted vengeance so badly. But that was before I'd opened my heart to God's forgiveness and made my peace with the killers.

The captain offered me the perfect revenge: trained and well-armed soldiers who would kill at my command. All I had to do was whisper a name and I could avenge my family . . . and the families of the thousands of corpses rotting in the street. His offer came from his heart, but I could hear the devil in his voice. He was tempting me with promises of murder, when all I wanted was peace. I slipped my hand into my pocket and wrapped my fingers around my father's rosary. "Thank you for offering to—"

"I'll kill any Hutu you want me to!" He was so eager to kill that he didn't let me finish my sentence. "If there's a Hutu you know about in this camp, tell me and I'll shoot them myself. I hate them all."

"Well, Hutus aren't evil, Captain, it's just these killers. They've been tricked by the devil . . . they've wandered away from God and—"

"Immaculée, Hutus *are* evil," he cut in again. "What they've done is evil. Don't tell me that this is God's will or the work of the devil—it's the work of the Hutus, and they'll pay for it. If you change your mind, let me know. I don't offer to kill for just anyone, you know."

I prayed that God would touch the captain's heart with His forgiveness, and I prayed again for the killers to put down their machetes and beg for God's mercy. The captain's anger made me think that the cycle of hatred and mistrust in Rwanda would not easily be broken. There would certainly be even more bitterness after the killing stopped, bitterness that could easily erupt into more violence. Only God's Divine forgiveness could stop that from happening now. I could see that whatever path God put me on, helping others to forgive would be a big part of my life's work.

The next day the captain proved good to his word—he really did hate Hutus. A bleeding man wandered into camp claiming to be a genocide survivor wounded while fighting with the Tutsi rebels, but the captain didn't believe him. The soldiers forced the man to his knees, pressing their guns to his head while they interrogated him. They asked him if he was a member of the Interahamwe, which at first he denied. But after more questioning, he broke down and confessed. The captain nodded to his soldiers, they dragged him away, and we never saw him again. One of the soldiers later told me that the man admitted to being an Interahamwe spy.

"Don't worry about him—he won't be bothering anyone ever again," he said.

I CARED FOR MY AUNTS AND NIECES AS BEST I COULD, ensuring that they had enough food, bringing them medicine from the soldiers, and tending to their wounds—I even made sure to sleep close to them in case they became frightened in the night. But I didn't spend as much time with them as one might think. I was happy that they were alive and safe, but they couldn't replace the family I'd lost. I felt that I had to start a new life.

It was even difficult for me to associate with the ladies I'd been in the bathroom with. We lived in opposite corners of the camp, and while we'd smile at each other, we rarely spoke. Although we'd been in such close quarters for so long, we didn't really know each other. All our communication had been through hand signals and lip reading, and it had almost always conveyed fear, terror, and desperation. Maybe we would have become friends if we'd been able to talk in the bathroom, but as it was, seeing each other in the camp brought back too many painful memories.

Anyway, there was plenty of opportunity to make new acquaintances. New groups of Tutsi survivors arrived every day, most of whom were confused and disoriented and spoke only Kinyarwanda. Because I was bilingual, the captain asked me to register all incoming refugees, and I was happy to help. I recorded their names and ages, and reported their injuries and medical needs to the French soldiers. I also wrote down their personal stories and a history of what they'd been though. Through this process, I heard many horrific tales, but made some lasting friendships.

One new pal was Florence, a young woman about my age with a sweet, innocent smile. She was very pretty, despite the deep scar running down her face from being chopped between the eyes with a machete. I jotted down her story, which, sadly, was as common as it was gruesome.

Florence was from a small town not far from my village. When the genocide began, her family and 300 of her neighbors sought asylum at their local chapel, thinking that the killers would respect the sanctity of the church. But finding Tutsis jammed together in one room only made it easier for the killers, who simply walked between the pews swinging their blades.

"We had no weapons, no way to defend ourselves," Florence said, her big, kind eyes filling with tears. "There was some screaming and begging, but most of us just sat there waiting for our turn to be slaughtered. It was like we thought that we deserved to be murdered—that it was all perfectly natural. They reached me, and all I can remember is the machete coming down toward my face. Then I woke up in the truck."

Florence's wound was deep, but not lethal—yet the killers had tossed her into the back of a big truck with the rest of the corpses. When she woke up, she discovered that she was on top of her parents' bodies, and her sister was on top of *her.*

"My sister had a spear still stuck in her chest . . . she was almost dead but still making gurgling noises. I tried to reach out to her, but one of the killers riding in the truck saw me move and started sticking me with his spear. He stuck me here, here, and here," she said, pointing to her chest, stomach, and thighs. "I didn't flinch when he stabbed me; instead, I asked God to take my pain and save my life. The killer must have thought that I was dead because I was bleeding so much."

The truck then stopped at the edge of a cliff high above the Akanyaru River, a favorite spot of the Interahamwe for dumping corpses.

"They threw all the bodies over the cliff and into the river," Florence continued. "I remember them grabbing me by my feet and swinging me into the air, and I heard the sound of the water rushing in the distance, but I don't remember falling. I woke up in the mud by the riverbank the next morning. My parents and sister were lying there, too, but they were all dead. I looked up at the cliff and couldn't imagine how I survived—it was at least a 200-foot drop. I can only believe that God spared me for something."

Florence lay by the riverbank for a day before she could get up and walk away. She stumbled to the nearest house where some kind Hutus took her in, dressed her wounds, and hid her. "Even though they saved my life," she continued, "their son left the house every morning, met with the Interahamwe, and kept killing Tutsis in my town until there were none left to kill. Nothing makes sense to me anymore, Immaculée. Why do you think I lived and my parents and sister didn't?"

"God has spared you for a reason," I answered. "I'm writing down your story, and someday someone will read it and know what happened. You're like me—you've been left to tell."

I DID A LOT OF TRANSLATING BETWEEN THE REFUGEES and our French hosts; consequently, I got to know quite a few of the soldiers. One of them, Pierre, took a special interest in me. He was assigned to patrol the inner circle of the camp during the day, but at night he'd pass the time chatting with me as I sat watching the stars.

Pierre was a very nice young man who was a few years younger than I was, and he was polite, empathetic, and a good listener. I told him what had happened to my family and our village, and he told me about his parents, his life in France, and the girlfriend he'd broken up with before coming to Rwanda. When he asked if I had a boyfriend, I told him about John and the empty-hearted way we'd left things.

I felt very comfortable around Pierre, and I enjoyed his company. Talking to him could get my mind off my daily reality, at least temporarily. As the days went by, Pierre began finding excuses to be near me: He'd bring me food, escort me to the stream to fetch water, and drop by with books for me to read. His friends kidded him about it, but I didn't mind. Having a close friend who wasn't directly suffering from the genocide was a relief, and telling him my hopes and dreams made me feel human again.

One day Pierre's friend Paul told me that the young soldier was smitten with me, which made me laugh. I hadn't changed my clothes or had a proper shower in more than three months.

"No, Pierre talks about you all the time," Paul assured me. "He says that despite everything you've been through, your heart is open and you have a great sense of humor."

"The way you guys are joking with me about this, I *have* to have a sense of humor," I said. But I soon came to realize that Paul wasn't kidding—Pierre did have a crush on me.

I was flattered, but not interested. I'd just lost my family, and I wasn't sure if I'd live to see the end of the war. I'd also given up on romance after John had let me down so badly. Even so, Pierre made me wonder if my broken heart could ever love another person again.

When he came calling that night, asking me to go for a walk, I resolved to tell him not to waste his affection on me. But he began speaking with such conviction and passion that I was caught off guard.

"You've become so much more to me than a friend, Immaculée," he earnestly told me. "You're a very special person. I know that with all the death, pain, and violence around us, this is the last thing you want to hear, but I think I love you. I want to be with you." Even though I was expecting him to say something along those lines, I was still surprised by how genuine he sounded.

"Pierre," I replied softly, "my heart is full of sorrow, and right now there's only room in there for God. I can't think of falling in love . . . and I can't lose focus on the struggles ahead. I have to take care of myself."

He took my hand. "But I mean what I say . . . I love you and will take care of you. I want to be with you, and I don't want to lose you."

I was a little overwhelmed by his intensity, but I felt that we'd been brought together by circumstance, not by God. He had let me know that John was not the man He had meant for me, and now He was letting me know that neither was Pierre. It just didn't feel right—and I knew that when I was ready, God would bring love to me. And when He did, there would be no doubts or misgivings.

"No, Pierre . . . no. Right now my heart belongs more to the dead than to the living—I haven't even begun to mourn yet. Your friendship means so much to me, and I want to keep it. So please, let's just be friends."

"I see," he said sadly. "If I can't have your heart, then I'll let you go. I'll say good-bye, and . . . goodnight, sweetheart." He bent toward me and surprised me by kissing me on the mouth. I closed my eyes, and for the brief moment that his lips touched mine, I felt the warmth of the kiss lift my pain and sadness. Pierre walked away to join the other soldiers, leaving me with a resigned smile on my face. I'd put my trust in God, which was the only thing to do.

I DESPERATELY WANTED TO TALK TO MY BROTHER AIMABLE and let him know that I was alive, but there was no mail service and the phones weren't working—and it's not as if I had a number for him or money to pay for the call. Aimable was 3,000 miles away studying in Senegal, and I prayed that he'd stayed there. If he'd come back to Rwanda, he was sure to be dead like the rest of my family. So the war would have to end before I'd be able to reach him.

But when would the war be over? The French didn't share news with us, and we had no radio we could listen to. The only news we received came from new arrivals to our increasingly crowded camp.

Toward the end of July, I did learn that the Tutsi rebels of the RPF had claimed victory in the north, but that fighting continued in the east and south. The French had control of western Rwanda, where we were, including the shore of Lake Kivu and the border of Zaire. It was good news for us, but the situation was still extremely dangerous. Hundreds of thousands of Hutu refugees were in our area trying to reach Lake Kivu and escape to Zaire.

Each day new Tutsi survivors were dropped at our gates. In the three weeks since I'd arrived at the camp, our number had grown from a couple dozen to nearly 150—and I continued to record their stories and medical conditions. Many of the refugees were severely wounded, missing limbs or maimed from other types of torture. Often their wounds had become badly infected, and I knew that they wouldn't survive. And those who hadn't lost limbs had often lost their minds, driven mad by loss, grief, and the horror locked in their memory.

Among the most difficult things for me to deal with at the camp were the orphans. For example, I'll never forget the two brothers, ages three and four, who came to us from Kigali. Their parents had hidden them in the ceiling of their house when killers arrived at their door. The parents were murdered, and the boys were retrieved a few days later by kindhearted Hutu neighbors who brought them south when they fled the capital to escape the fighting. They delivered the boys to some French soldiers, explaining that they were about to cross into Zaire, which was too perilous a journey for the children.

For some reason the soldiers hadn't taken down the names of the children or the neighbors. In addition, both boys were running high fevers when they arrived at our camp. They were the youngest children in the camp, with no parent or relative to mind them, so I temporarily adopted and cared for them. With the French captain's help, I set up a bed for them inside the schoolhouse and got medicine to bring their fever down.

It broke my heart to listen to them talk. They'd seen their parents' corpses but were too young to understand the permanence of death. The older boy tried to take care of his younger brother by reminding him to be polite to strangers. The three-year-old kept pestering his big brother for French fries and soda, and the big brother would always reply with gentle patience.

"You have to remember that we're not home . . . we can't get French fries or soda here. We have to wait for Mommy and Daddy to come get us—then we can have treats again. We can't act spoiled, or more bad things will happen." When his little brother cried, he cradled him, saying, "Don't cry . . . Mommy and Daddy will be here soon, and then you can have all the French fries you want. We have to wait, but Mommy and Daddy will make everything okay."

I knew that those boys would never see their parents again, and that in all likelihood, *all* their relatives were dead. I feared that their future would be filled with sadness, abuse, and denied opportunities —the kind of lives where bitterness and hatred easily take root.

I saw the circle of hatred and mistrust forming in those innocent eyes, and I knew that God was showing me another reason He'd spared me. I vowed that one day, when I was strong and capable enough, I would do everything I could to help the children orphaned by the genocide. I would try to bring hope and happiness to their lives, and to steer them away from embracing the hatred that had robbed them of their parents, and of a family's love.

AT THE BEGINNING OF AUGUST, THE CAPTAIN TOLD ME the camp was so full that he was going to move the majority of the refugees. The new camp was indoors, in a high school in Kibuye town, with running water, better food, and real beds. I made sure "my" boys were the first to go so that they could be more comfortable. I also made sure that my aunts and cousins were transferred—yes, they were doing better, but they needed a roof over their heads, and walls around them, to make them feel more secure. I was planning to go myself and take care of everybody, but the captain begged me to remain behind and help run the camp. They still needed a translator, and there were new survivors coming in all the time.

"You'll help save lives if you stay," he told me. How could I refuse? I stayed on at the camp, and I never saw the little brothers again. But I didn't forget my promise to take care of other children orphaned by violence, which there was never any shortage of in Rwanda.

About 30 refugees remained in the old camp, including 8 friends I'd made, such as Florence and Jean Paul. Our small group had become quite close and felt like a little family. In fact, our bond was so tight that all nine of us refused to be transferred from the camp unless we were allowed to leave as a group.

We continued to receive Tutsi refugees, but the camp was now running like a transit station. I registered survivors, and within a day or two they were transferred to the larger camp in town. And then, in early August I was privy to something I hadn't heard in months: deep, rumbling, hearty laughter. It was coming from a woman who'd arrived with the new batch of refugees. She was sitting in a wheelchair, and the soldiers were lifting her down from the truck. She was a heavy woman, and her legs were so withered that I could see she'd never be able to walk. I wondered what on earth she had to laugh about in the midst of so much sadness. As it turned out, she was laughing at the joy of being alive.

I watched as the soldiers carefully set her wheelchair on the ground and then handed her two young children. The kids kissed her all over her face, and she began laughing again—and it echoed through the camp.

"That's Aloise," said Jean Paul. "We have a celebrity in the camp."

Indeed, I'd heard of Aloise. My parents had spoken highly of her to me when I was a child as an example of how far a person can go in life with hard work and determination. They'd told me that Aloise had contracted polio when she was nine and had never walked again, but she'd maintained high grades in school and was considered to be one of the brightest students in Rwanda. That was all I could remember hearing about her, but apparently she'd become quite famous in the country—many people in the camp had heard of her.

Jean Paul told me that her husband worked at the United Nations in Kigali, and Aloise had gotten to know all the diplomats and ambassadors. "She's connected to everyone and can get anyone a good job," he said with admiration. "People say that if she wasn't handicapped, she'd have become prime minister. I know she's a Tutsi, but she bought a Hutu identity card years ago so that she could get government contracts . . . she's a very smart lady."

"Well, I guess I'll go and register our famous guest," I said, and headed over to the truck with my notebook.

Aloise looked up at me from her wheelchair. Her mirth stopped abruptly, and she burst into tears. "Oh, my God, I can see your mother's face in yours . . . and your father's, too. I always wanted to visit you and your family, but I couldn't, not with these legs."

I thought the woman was mad or had mistaken me for someone else. I'd never met her, so how could she know who I was?

"Don't look at me like I've lost my mind, Immaculée Ilibagiza. I know very well who you are. Your parents—God rest their souls—were very good friends of mine." Aloise set her children down, wiped away her tears, and held her arms out to me.

I approached her tentatively, offering my hand for her to shake, but she grabbed my arm, pulled me to her, and gave me a mighty squeeze. She wouldn't let go. "Your mother saved my life—I bet you didn't know that! When I was eight years old, your mom heard that I loved school but that my parents couldn't afford to send me anymore. Well, she paid for my whole year's schooling . . . and she kept paying, even after I got sick and couldn't walk anymore. I was so grateful that I promised to make something of my life and studied harder than any-one I knew. Everything I have today I owe to your mother, Immaculée. She was a saint!"

Aloise finally released me from her long embrace, and I staggered backward. I was flabbergasted by my strange encounter with this overpowering woman, and I needed to step away to regain my com-posure. "Let me get some food and water for you and your children," I said. "I'll come right back, and then I can register you."

As I was walking away, Aloise called out, "Immaculée, I think your mother's spirit brought me here for you! I owe her a debt, and I'm going to repay it by helping you. Let me think about it . . . I'll come up with a way to help you out."

I waved at her and kept walking, wondering what a refugee in a wheelchair with two young children to care for could possibly do to help me. Once again, I was to learn that God moves in mysterious ways.

When I registered Aloise the next day, she told me that although she was legally a Hutu, her husband, Fari, was a Tutsi. That meant that her children, Sami and Kenza, were considered Tutsi as well. She feared for the children's safety and fled their Kigali home to hide at her parents' house. Her husband had been concealed in their ceiling when she left, and she had no idea if he was dead or alive.

"I've decided what I can do for you to repay your mother's

kindness," Aloise said. "As soon as the fighting is completely over, I'm taking you home with me to Kigali. You can live with us like you're our own daughter."

There was something I didn't quite trust about Aloise. I smiled at her and thanked her for the offer, but told her that I had a little family of friends in the camp and that we'd promised to stick together. She shrugged her shoulders and said that I was wise to stay with people I trusted. I thought that was the end of it, but the next day she came over to me while I was sitting with my friends.

"Immaculée, I've thought it over and decided that if you're worried, I'm going to kidnap you; you can bring all your friends with you to Kigali. I'll put all nine of you up at my house! It will be cozy, but we'll make room."

We looked at each other and laughed. We didn't know how to reply to such a strange and generous offer.

"Think about it," Aloise said, wheeling away in her chair. "I don't know what else you think you can do after the war. You all must be traumatized . . . I can't believe I have to beg you kids to come live in a nice house in the city. The war is almost over—start thinking about your future!"

Aloise was right. The capital had fallen to the rebels, and it was only a matter of time before the fighting ended. We'd all lost our families, our homes, even our clothes, and we didn't have a penny among us. It didn't take long for us to decide it was a good idea to accept Aloise's offer. The next day, we went as a group to accept her offer and thank her.

"Don't thank me, thank Immaculée's mother," she said. "I'm doing this for Rose, not for you!"

She began chuckling, and kept on until, once again, peals of happy, heartfelt laughter echoed throughout the camp.

><

CHAPTER 20

The Road to the Rebels

On a hot afternoon in late August, the French captain notified me that we were being evicted. Operation Turquoise was wrapping up, so the French were preparing to leave Rwanda. "We're shutting down our camp today," he said. "You have two hours to get everyone ready to leave."

"Leave for where?" I asked. "There are 30 people here . . . where should I tell them to go? We have no homes!" I was stunned by the sudden news.

"We're taking you all to stay with Tutsi soldiers. The RPF has moved into the area and set up camp a few miles down the road. We'll take you there and hand you over to them. It will be better for you, since you'll be with your own people."

I was thrilled to hear that the Tutsi soldiers had finally fought their way to us and were chasing the Interahamwe right out of the country. I even heard that our hero, RPF leader Paul Kagame, had set up a new government in Kigali. Thank God, we were finally safe—the genocide must really be over!

I moved through the camp telling everyone that we were leaving. Some of the newest arrivals were dubious, saying that the French were not to be trusted and that they'd set up refugee camps as humanitarian fronts to help cover up their real mission: smuggling the Hutus who'd organized the genocide across Lake Kivu and safely out of Rwanda.

"I don't believe it," I said. "The French have kept us safe for weeks, and they're about to deliver us to freedom! They've done everything they said they would do."

It didn't take long to get ready, since we'd been prepared for a long time. No one owned anything, so we had no luggage to pack. I gathered up my meager belongings—the sweater and towel that Pastor Murinzi's daughter had given me, two books from Pierre, and some extra soap and T-shirts from the soldiers—and put them into a plastic bag. But as I did, I thought of my mother packing her things in suitcases while the killers gathered near our home . . . and I decided that I didn't want to drag things from my past into my new life. I wanted to make a clean break. I took the bag into the schoolhouse and left it in a corner, hoping that some other poor, homeless Tutsi would find it.

I turned to leave and bumped into Pierre, who was standing in the doorway. He looked at me forlornly and handed me a piece of paper. "This is my address in France, in case you ever change your mind. I will miss you terribly and will keep you in my heart. I pray that God keeps you safe."

"Good-bye, Pierre. God bless you," I said, but he was already gone.

I WAS THE LAST ONE TO CLIMB INTO THE BACK OF THE TRUCK. The tailgate slammed shut, the canvas tarp was rolled down to conceal us, and the truck rolled forward. I took out the rosary my father had given me—the one possession I would never surrender—and said a prayer. I asked God for His blessing on our new beginning, and to shepherd us safely to the Tutsi soldiers.

The truck pulled past the semicircle of armored vehicles, down a service road, and into a sea of killers! Through a crack in the tarp, I saw that thousands of Hutus were trudging along the main road toward Lake Kivu—and hundreds of them wore the uniform of the Interahamwe and carried machetes.

"Oh, God," I said, falling back in the truck. "Not again!"

We inched along the crowded road, honking at Hutus to give way and let us by. I knew that if we were stopped, or if the truck broke down, the Interahamwe would fall upon us within minutes. I hadn't felt this frightened since I left the bathroom.

"Please, God," I prayed. "You have brought us this far—now take us the rest of the way! Blind these killers . . . don't let them look in the back of this truck. Merciful God, shield us from their hateful eyes!"

We were more than halfway to the RPF camp when the truck stopped. The French captain came around to the back, pulled the tarp open, and said, "We have reports of gunfire in the area, and we have orders to avoid fighting at any cost. We're turning around, so this is where you'll have to get out."

I thought I'd misheard him. "You mean that you're taking us back with you, right?"

"No, we're breaking camp. You have to get out here . . . now. I'm sorry, Immaculée."

I'd gotten to know the captain well over the past few weeks. He hated the Hutu killers and said that he wanted to help the Tutsis in any way he could, so I couldn't believe that he'd leave us in a group of armed Interahamwe. I climbed out of the truck to reason with him. "Please, Captain, you know better than anyone what will happen if you leave us here. There are killers all around us! Please, I'm begging you . . . take us another mile to the RPF camp, or take us back with you . . . don't leave us here to be killed!"

"I'm sorry, Immaculée. I have my orders."

"Please, Captain, just take us—"

"*No!* Now get your people out of the back. We have to leave."

We couldn't believe what was happening. A dozen or so Interahamwe were standing about ten feet away, watching us and listening to our conversation with growing interest. I felt dizzy, the road was spinning, and all I could see for a moment was a blur of angry faces. I steadied myself on the side of the truck, and for the first time noticed all the bodies on the ground—corpses everywhere along the road, as far as I could see.

I looked up at the captain, pleading with my eyes one last time. It was useless—he was immovable. Perhaps the pastor and the others had been right about the French. Maybe they really were here to help the killers, because they were certainly about to leave us for dead.

"Get out of the truck," I said to my friends. "Everybody out . . . the French are leaving us here."

The cries of disbelief and fear coming from the back of the truck drew even more attention from the killers, who were now moving toward us. I looked one Interahamwe straight in the eye and held his gaze. My heart told me that he was a person just like me, and that he

171

really didn't want to kill. I held my rosary and summoned all my will to send a message of love to him. I prayed that God would use me to touch the killer with the power of His love.

I didn't blink . . . and we stared into each other's eyes for what seemed like a lifetime. Finally, the killer broke my gaze and looked away. He turned his back to me and dropped his machete, as if the devil had left his body. But there were plenty of other devils to take his place. At least 15 Interahamwe were now standing a few yards from the truck, with machetes in their hands and smirks on their faces. They were figuring out what was happening, waiting to see if any of my companions would dare leave the truck.

We had no choice but to come out. One by one, my friends hopped out, until all 30 of us were standing there facing the killers. When everyone was out, two French soldiers lifted Aloise down onto the road and deposited young Kenza and Sami beside her. Then the soldiers climbed into the cab, and the truck pulled away at high speed, leaving us in a cloud of dust and uncertainty.

"Look at all these Tutsis," one of the killers said in amazement. "How can it be that they're still alive?"

"These are the cockroaches that the French soldiers were protecting," another said. "Who's going to save you now, cockroaches?"

My friends were so scared that they could barely move. They nudged me, asking me what we should do, as though I were somehow an expert in dealing with ruthless killers. I looked at the machete scar on Florence's face, remembering the story she told me about sitting in a church with her family, waiting their turn for the killers to chop them to death. Well, I wasn't going to stand around and wait to die.

"Let's go," I said. "We'll walk to the RPF camp—their soldiers are close by."

The killers heard me mention the RPF and got nervous.

We began moving but didn't get too far. The road was so strewn with rocks and bodies that it was practically impossible to push Aloise's wheelchair—so when a wheel became stuck in a rut, we all stopped. Aloise's children were also crying and clutching their mother's arms.

I pulled my friends Jean Paul and Karega away from the group. "You two come with me—the rest of you stay with Aloise . . . and pray. I'll find the Tutsi soldiers and come back with help. Don't move from this spot or I won't be able to find you in the middle of all these Hutu refugees."

Aloise looked at me doubtfully. "Are you sure you want to go? They'll kill you for sure! Let the men go instead," she implored.

"No, I'm going . . . you just concentrate on praying."

With that, I struck out in the direction that the French had been taking us before they abandoned us. As we walked, I prayed my rosary, talking to God with all my heart and soul: "God, I really am walking through the valley of death—please stay with me. Shield me with the power of Your love. You created this ground that we're walking on, so please don't let these killers spill Your daughter's blood on it."

Three Interahamwe followed us as we broke away from the larger group, and one of them recognized me. "I know this cockroach," he said. "This is Leonard's daughter—we've been looking for her for months! I can't believe she's still alive . . . we killed the rest of them, but this little cockroach gave us the slip!"

"Dear God," I prayed, walking as fast as I could and holding my father's rosary tightly in my hand. "Only You can save me. You promised to take care of me, God—well, I really need taking care of right now. There are devils and vultures at my back, Lord . . . please protect me. Take the evil from the hearts of these men, and blind their hatred with Your holy love."

I walked without looking at my feet, not knowing if I was about to stumble over rocks or bodies, putting all my trust in God to guide me to safety. We were moving very briskly, but the killers were all around us now, circling us, slicing the air with their machetes. We were defenseless, so why were they waiting to strike?

"If they kill me, God, I ask You to forgive them. Their hearts have been corrupted by hatred, and they don't know why they want to hurt me."

After walking a half mile like that, I heard Jean Paul say, "Hey, they're gone . . . they're gone!"

I looked around, and it was true—the killers had left us. Jean Paul said later that it was probably because they knew the RPF soldiers were close by, but I knew the real reason, and I never stopped thanking God for saving us on that road!

A few minutes later we saw an RPF roadblock and several dozen tall, lean, stone-faced Tutsi soldiers standing guard. I broke into an all-out run and dropped to my knees in front of them. I closed my eyes and sang their praises.

"Thank God, thank God, we're saved! Thank God you're here. Bless you, bless you all! If only you knew what we've been through. Thank you for—"

I didn't get a chance to finish my sentence because I was cut off by the chilling, metallic sound of a machine-gun bolt being pulled back. I opened my eyes, only to see that the barrel of the gun was an inch from my face.

≫◄

CHAPTER 21

On to Kigali

*O*h, God, when will You put an end to this nightmare?

I looked over the gun barrel and into the cold, angry eyes of a Tutsi soldier. They reminded me of the killer's eyes I'd stared down not 20 minutes before.

If these were the same RPF soldiers we'd been hoping would rescue us since the genocide began, then maybe it really was my time to die. My neighbors had turned on me, the killers were hunting me, the French had abandoned me, and now my Tutsi saviors were preparing to blow my brains out.

It's up to You, God, I prayed silently. *Live or die, it doesn't matter to me as long as I'm serving Your will. You have brought me here—it's up to You to decide.*

I tried to get to my feet, slowly raising my hands in the air while explaining that my two friends and I were Tutsis: "The French soldiers left us in the road . . . there are other survivors of the genocide back there surrounded by killers. Please, you've got to go help them before it's too late."

"Shut your mouth and sit on the ground!" the soldier shouted, poking me with his rifle.

"If you're Tutsis, why are you still alive?!" a different one screamed, pointing his gun at me. "Everyone is dead, *everyone!* You're killers yourselves . . . you're Hutu spies! Do you know what we do to spies? Sit still—don't say a word, and don't move a muscle."

Angry soldiers surrounded us, so there was no point in talking. I kept my mouth shut and waited for whatever destiny had in store for me. Minutes passed . . . I thought about Aloise and the others sitting in the field of killers, waiting for me to keep my promise and send soldiers to save them. God help them.

Eventually the rebel commander arrived to question us. The soldiers guarding us saluted him and called him "Major." He was tall, skinny as a stick, and one of the calmest-looking people I'd ever seen. He looked at us like we were thieves who'd been caught breaking into his house . . . and he had the same expression on his face that the French soldiers did when they caught the Interahamwe spy. I crossed myself, remembering what had happened to that man. It was obvious that the major didn't believe that we were genocide survivors, so I began praying for the poor souls we'd left by the roadside.

But of course, that's when God stepped in once again.

"Immaculée? *Immaculée Ilibagiza?*" A soldier standing beside the major was saying my name and staring at me in disbelief. "Immaculée! It can't be you, can it? Is it really you?"

"Bazil?"

"It *is* you!" He dropped his rifle, knelt to the ground, and gave me a big hug.

Bazil was a Hutu neighbor who'd gone to fight with the Tutsi rebels. We'd known each other since school, and he'd been my mother's favorite student for many years because he was so bright and gifted. We called him "teacher's pet" because Mom liked him so much that she'd invited him to the house many times.

"You know this girl?" the major asked when Bazil finished embracing me.

"Oh yes, we went to school together. Her parents are very respected Tutsis in my village—they're very good people. She's all right, Major . . . she's not a spy. Whatever Immaculée says is true."

I quickly thanked God for sending Bazil at the very moment I needed him. The soldiers lowered their guns, and the major reached out and shook my hand. "I'm Major Ntwali," he said. "I'm sorry about the confusion, but there are spies everywhere. It's still very dangerous around here, but you're safe with us. The war is over for you . . . we'll protect you from now on."

"Thank you, Major, but my friends are the ones who need your protection," I explained urgently. "The French soldiers left us in the middle of the Interahamwe, and a half mile down the road there are 30 Tutsi survivors with killers all around. I don't even know if they're still alive. Please—"

The major had signaled for someone to fetch Aloise and the others before I'd finished speaking. "Don't worry about your friends. We'll get to them."

"Thank you . . . and God bless you!"

After the soldiers left to help the others, Bazil sat down next to me and anxiously peppered me with questions: "I haven't been home in months . . . do you have news from the village? How is Teacher—I mean, your mom? Any news about my parents, or my brothers and sisters? The last time I saw them they were going to leave the country . . . did they get out?"

I put my hand on Bazil's arm. I knew the pain I was about to cause him, so I tried to be as gentle as possible. "I don't know how to tell you this, Bazil, other than to tell you the truth. Everyone is dead: my family, your family . . . almost every Tutsi and moderate Hutu in our village—they're all dead."

He looked at me as if he'd forgotten how to speak, and then he crumpled into a ball at my feet, his chest heaving in spasms as he sobbed onto the butt of his rifle. Poor Bazil . . . he'd lost his parents, four brothers, and three sisters.

I understood now why we'd been treated with such suspicion when we arrived. Many of these soldiers had been fighting their way down from Uganda and had no news from home along the way. They were now returning to find their families slaughtered by neighbors—people they'd trusted all their lives. There was not much happiness in the rebel camp.

I wasn't feeling much happiness at the moment either. I felt heartsick for giving the news to Bazil, and as the minutes passed, I feared that the worst had befallen Aloise and the group. I prayed hard for their safety, and soon I heard my merry friend's familiar laughter coming from an approaching RPF truck.

"Whatever prayers you've been saying, keep on saying them, Immaculée," Aloise chuckled. "Those killers were looking at us like they wanted to cut us to pieces, but they couldn't move. It was as though they were frozen to the spot! We were like Daniel in the lions' den . . . just like Daniel in the lions' den!"

Aloise pulled her children to her, hugged them tightly, and laughed and laughed until tears ran down her cheeks. My heart lifted, and I said, "I didn't know if I'd ever live to say this, but we'll never have to face the killers again. The genocide is over—God has spared us and given us a new life. Praise the Lord! Thank You, God! *Thank You, God!*"

Aloise smiled at me and said, "Amen, Immaculée . . . Amen!"

ALOISE'S SUNNY DISPOSITION AND INDEPENDENT SPIRIT charmed the hardened soldiers. She spent the first few hours at camp amusing them with stories about the famous people she'd met, and then she kept them laughing with her bawdy jokes. But they were most impressed with her unbeatable optimism: She never complained about her lot in life, and she made the most of every situation, no matter how difficult.

Aloise and I got along so well that Major Ntwali asked if she were my mother. "No," I replied, "but she treats me like a daughter. My parents and two of my brothers were actually killed in the genocide—so were most of my other relatives."

"I'm sorry," the major said. "Do you blame us?"

"What do you mean?" I asked, confused by the question.

"A lot of my soldiers blame themselves for what happened. They think that we spent too much time fighting to take over Kigali while hundreds of thousands of Tutsi were being killed, including their own families. They think we took too long to get here."

"They shouldn't think like that, Major—it's not your fault. You fought to save us . . . you fought the devil. Now we have to make sure we never face the same battle. We have to stop killing and learn to forgive."

He shook his head at me, clucking his tongue in disapproval. "Don't talk to me about God or the devil—I know who did this. You can forgive all you want to, Immaculée, but maybe you haven't looked into as many mass graves as I have. The people who filled those graves are still out there, and believe me, they don't deserve your forgiveness. They deserve to be shot, and I intend to give them what they deserve. I'll forgive them when they're dead."

The major pointed to a nearby Baptist church. "You'll find other survivors in there. Stay put until we figure out what to do with you, and don't wander off. Remember, you're still in a war zone. If you run into some Interahamwe, they won't be as forgiving as you are."

My little group and I stayed in the church with about 100 other Tutsi survivors. There were no beds or blankets, but we were happy to have a roof over our heads, and it felt good to be in a house of God. Bazil had food to give us, which I volunteered to cook. But as I tried to light a cooking fire outside, I felt nauseated by a sickening stench.

"What in the Lord's name is that smell?" I asked one of the soldiers posted to stand guard over us. He took me by the hand, and without saying a word, led me behind the church. It was an image from hell: row upon row of corpses, hundreds and hundreds of them stacked up like firewood. A black carpet of flies hovered about them, and crows picked at the top layer of the dead. An old man stood at the edge of the pile shooing away dogs with a stick.

I covered my mouth, my eyes wide in horror. Then the soldier pointed beyond the piles to a deep pit at least 30 yards across and 20 feet deep. It was filled with bodies, maybe tens of thousands of them. I turned my head, vomited, and staggered back to the front of the church. The soldier followed me, still saying nothing.

"Are you from this area?" I asked. He nodded, and I understood then that somewhere in that rotting pit of humanity was his family. His pain was beyond words.

How many years—how many generations—would it take before Rwanda could recover from such horror? How long for our wounded hearts to heal, for our hardened hearts to soften? Too long for me, I decided. Looking into that soldier's eyes, I realized that I was going to have to leave Rwanda.

I'd have to leave the sorrow and suffering of this country behind, at least for a while. In order to help heal others, as I knew God wanted me to, I needed the perspective that only space and time could provide. I had to first heal myself to be able to assist the others: the orphans at the French camp, the major whose heart harbored vengeance, the killers who still had murder in their eyes, and the soldier before me whose grief was smothering his soul.

I would leave, but not yet. I had much to do first, and besides, I had no job, no money, and no prospects. All I owned were the clothes on my back and my father's rosary in my pocket.

WE STAYED WITH THE REBEL SOLDIERS FOR A FEW DAYS, spending most of our time trying to figure out how we could get to Kigali without any money. All 12 of us could stay at Aloise's house once we got there, but we had no way of making the still-dangerous, five-hour journey. I prayed for days about it and asked everyone to do the same. Eventually God answered and sent Major Ntwali to see us with the solution.

The major offered us a truck and driver to take us right to Aloise's front door. Not only that, but when the truck picked us up, the major had his soldiers load it with sacks of rice, flour, sugar, beans, coffee, tins of milk, and cans of oil. It was more food than I'd seen in months, more than enough to last us for months. We thanked the major repeatedly for his generosity as we waved good-bye and headed off for Kigali.

We arrived in the capital in the middle of what would have been a busy working day a few months earlier. As it was, we drove into a ghost town. The streets were deserted except for the occasional United Nations truck or RPF Jeep darting along the empty roads, swerving to avoid the corpses in the street . . . or the carcasses of the hundreds of dogs the soldiers had shot to stop them from scavenging on human remains. The air reeked of death, and I could hear the wind shrieking through abandoned homes like evicted spirits. So many buildings lay in ruins, burned out and pockmarked by machine-gun fire and mortar rounds. Shop doors were ripped from their hinges, the stores were looted, and every once in a while we'd hear an explosion in the distance. I couldn't recognize the beautiful city whose bright lights and busy boulevards had thrilled me so much as a teenager.

"Watch where you step," our driver warned. "There are land mines everywhere . . . we can't remember where we put them all. You could go for a walk around here and end up without your legs."

We drove straight to the United Nations headquarters to see if we could find Aloise's husband, Fari. As she said, "It's only a 15-minute walk from our house to the UN. If he survived hiding in our ceiling, this is where he would have come. It's the safest place in Kigali."

We parked in front of the big metal gate and lifted Aloise out of the truck. She was shaking—it was the first time since meeting her that I'd seen her spirit falter. "I don't know how I'll go on if Fari was killed," she admitted. "He is my heart and soul, and he gives me my strength. I've prayed so hard for him to be alive . . . I hope God listens to my prayers the way He listens to you, Immaculée."

God did listen to Aloise's prayers. No sooner had she finished speaking than she spotted a familiar figure walking across the compound. "Oh, my God . . . that's him! I'm sure that's him—I'd recognize his walk anywhere. Call him, somebody call to him!"

We pleaded with one of the UN guards to run and get the man Aloise pointed out. The man walked toward us cautiously until he saw Aloise . . . and then he began running as fast as he could. He pushed through the gate, dropped to his knees, and began kissing her. "My darling, my darling," he said. Little Kenza and Sami jumped into his arms, smothering him with hugs and kisses. It was one of the happiest family reunions I'd ever seen, until Fari asked, "Where is the baby?"

Aloise's eyes filled with tears. "God took her," she croaked. "She had a fever and didn't make it."

Fari put his head into Aloise's lap and they cried for 15 or 20 minutes, while the rest of us stood around awkwardly, looking at each other. None of us knew that Aloise had lost a child before reaching the French camp. We marveled at her strength.

Eventually, Fari looked up and asked her who we were. "Orphans I adopted at the refugee camp," Aloise told him. "They'll be staying with us."

"You're all welcome," Fari said.

"The tall one there is the daughter of Rose and Leonard . . . both of our old friends are dead."

"Oh my," Fari said, getting up and taking my hand. "I see your parents in you, young lady. Be strong—your mom and dad were beautiful, kind people. God has spared you for a reason . . . you can stay with us until you find out what that reason is."

I didn't know what to say except "Thank you."

WE CLIMBED BACK INTO THE TRUCK AND DROVE to Aloise's house. On the way, Fari told us that he'd abandoned their home and had been living at the UN for the past four months. "If Aloise hadn't returned to me with the children," he said, "I would never have come back here. A home is a prison without love."

The place was a mess: The windows had been blown out, the walls were riddled with bullet holes, and part of the roof had caved in. Yet we all pitched in, spending the next week repairing and cleaning the house. With hard work, and construction materials we scrounged from several destroyed buildings, the place soon looked like a home again. Jean Paul and the other boys had their own rooms, while Florence and I became roommates. For the first time since I'd left my parents' house, I was able to sleep in a real bed. We were all in heaven!

While we had the food that Major Ntwali had supplied us with, we had no money—and after months of constant wear, our clothes were practically worn to threads. So we went to abandoned homes looking for shoes and newer things to wear. In one house I found a pair of gold earrings. I convinced myself that I deserved something pretty to make me feel good after all I'd been through, and I put them in my pocket. But when I tried them on in front of a mirror at Aloise's, I couldn't bear my own reflection. All I could see was the face of the woman who had owned them. The earrings didn't belong to me and held none of my memories; someone else had worked hard for them or had received them as a loving gift. I felt like a trespasser in another person's life. I didn't want possessions I hadn't earned and didn't deserve, so the next day I took the earrings back to where I'd found them.

Meanwhile, a little voice was whispering in my head, and I nodded in agreement with what I heard: *It is time for me to move on. It is time to get a job.*

≫◄

CHAPTER 22

The Lord's Work

God only knew where I would find a job in a city where people were afraid to walk the streets. Leftover land mines littered the streets of Kigali, but if I wanted to work, I had to pound the pavement. The buses weren't running, and I had no money for taxis.

I asked Fari if he knew of any businesses within walking distance that had any job openings. "Your options are pretty limited because nobody is hiring now," he replied. "The only possibility is the United Nations . . . but the people they hire usually have to speak English."

My mind snapped to attention. Of course! After all, the United Nations was the reason God had led me to study English in the bathroom in the first place. I'd even had a vision of working in a UN office.

I washed my clothes especially thoroughly that night and prayed hard for God to help me find a job at the United Nations. I was so excited about finally putting my English to use that I stayed up most of the night looking in the mirror, practicing the phrases I'd taught myself:

"Good morning to you."
"How do you do?"
"I am looking for a job."
"My name is Immaculée Ilibagiza."
"I am Rwandan."
"I studied science at the university in Butare."
"I am looking for a job."

Oh, how thrilling! I was speaking real English sentences, and to-morrow I'd have a real conversation in the new language . . . and by the end of the day I could be working at my new job! Praise God!

I was standing in front of the gate of the UN building at 8 A.M. sharp. A Ghanaian guard greeted me warmly in what sounded like English. I'm sure he said something like "Good morning, how can I help you?" But what I heard was "Blah, blah, blah, blah, blah?" I didn't have a clue what he was saying, but pretended I did. I held my head up, stuck my chin out, and said, "How do you do? My name is Immaculée Ilibagiza. I am looking for a job."

Ouch. The look in his eyes told me how ridiculous I must have sounded. Nevertheless, I tried again. I hadn't come this far to be turned away. "How do you do? My name is Immaculée. I am looking for a job."

"Ah! You're Rwandan . . . you must speak French," he said. I smiled and nodded. He opened the gate, and another guard escorted me to a small waiting room, where I filled out a lot of forms and was told to wait. So I waited . . . and waited . . . and waited . . . and waited. When the UN employees started leaving at the end of the day, I asked the receptionist how much longer I'd have to wait to get my job.

"You'll be waiting a long time, dear. There are no jobs."

I went home disappointed but not discouraged. It was my des-tiny to work at the UN—I had envisioned it and I was determined. If God wanted me to work there, nothing could stop me from reach-ing my goal.

I returned the next day, filled out the same forms, and again wait-ed all afternoon. I did the same thing the following day, and the day after that, and the day after that. I spent more than two weeks filling out forms and waiting. Every day the receptionist told me as I left, "I wouldn't bother coming back if I were you, dear. There are no jobs."

By the end of the second week, I *was* getting discouraged. I dread-ed going back to Aloise's without a job, so I wandered the battered streets of our Kigali neighborhood feeling sorry for myself. I wanted to sit in quiet communication with God to focus my energies, but Aloise's house was too noisy for me to meditate. Believe it or not, I actually longed for the days in the pastor's bathroom, when I could talk to God for hours without interruption. I remembered the joy and peace He filled my heart with during those long stretches of silent prayer, along with the mental clarity I enjoyed afterward.

Two blocks from Aloise's, I walked into the shell of a burned-out house, dropped to my knees on top of the charred rubble and broken glass, and began to pray: "Dear God, in the Bible, Peter was discouraged after fishing all night and catching nothing, but You told him to go fish again in the same spot—and he caught so many fish! He was so happy! Well, You guided me to the UN, and I've been 'fishing' for a job for days . . . but there are no fish here. God, I don't know what to do. I have no money, my clothes are falling apart, and they won't give me a job. So I need Your help. Let's make these UN people notice me and give me a good office job; You know how badly I need it. Help me, and I will help myself! Amen."

I BRUSHED MYSELF OFF AND LEFT THE RUINED HOME with renewed confidence. I'd asked God for His help, and now I knew it was up to me to make it happen. I began visualizing that I was already working at the UN, taking notes, answering phones, and helping make important decisions.

As I walked home, I thought about the things I'd need once the UN job was offered to me. I'd have to get some presentable clothes, and I'd definitely need my high school diploma and proof that I'd attended university for three years. Unfortunately, all my belongings were in my dorm room in Butare, which was a four-hour drive away, and I obviously had no money to pay for a taxi to take me there.

Since I was so lost in thought, I almost didn't notice a car pulling up beside me and the driver calling out my name. It was Dr. Abel, a professor from my university in Butare. "I hardly recognized you, Immaculée," he said. "You're so skinny! I'm so happy you've survived . . . but are you eating, and do you have a place to live?"

Dr. Abel was a medical doctor, so he asked me all sorts of questions about what I'd been through and about my health. He invited me to come live with his wife and family in Butare so that I could build up my strength. I thanked him, but explained that I already had a family to stay with. But if he were driving to Butare in the near future, I'd gladly accept a lift.

"Of course. In fact, I'm leaving tomorrow."

Again, I saw God's hand at work in what I'd thought was a chance encounter. The next day Dr. Abel dropped me off at the front gate of my old university. The school had been looted, and soldiers were posted at the gate. They refused to let me go to my room, saying, "The school is off limits indefinitely." Then they told me to go back to Kigali.

I sat at the side of the road and prayed with my father's rosary, waiting for God to show me how He was going to get me onto campus. Within ten minutes a car carrying an army colonel stopped at the gate. While the soldiers fell over each other trying to salute him, I walked up to the car and introduced myself.

"What are you doing here, little girl?" he replied. "Where are your parents? It's dangerous for you to be out here by yourself."

I was 24, but I'd lost so much weight that I looked more like a 12-year-old.

"My parents are dead, sir. They were killed with the rest of my family in the genocide. All I have left in the world is in my dorm room, but your soldiers won't let me into the school. Will you help me?" I asked as sweetly as possible.

The colonel opened the door, and I got in along with one of the soldiers. We drove through the gate and made the short, depressing drive to my dorm.

The beautiful campus where I'd formed so many wonderful memories and loving friendships was no more. There was garbage everywhere, and many of the buildings were charred and crumbling. Student records blew across the campus like tumbleweeds, and after all these weeks, there were still so many bodies on the ground. I couldn't bear to look, fearing that I'd see the corpse of Sarah or one of my other dear girlfriends. I tried to conjure the memory of the school dances I'd enjoyed, the plays I'd performed in, the romantic walks I'd taken with John . . . but all were obliterated by the devastation I saw before me.

The colonel dropped me at my dorm, and the soldier followed me to my room, which had been thoroughly plundered. The door had been smashed in with an ax, and everything I owned was gone—my suitcases, clothes, shoes, and even my mattress were all stolen. Thankfully, a few pictures of my parents were still hanging on the walls—my only mementos of our life together. I picked up a few scattered envelopes from the floor, but the soldier grabbed them from my hands and began reading them. He slung his rifle off his shoulder and demanded rather menacingly, "Who's Aimable?"

To his surprise, I started laughing. It struck me as funny that I'd survived the genocide, but could end up being shot by a Tutsi soldier for looting my empty dorm room.

"Aimable is my brother. That letter was mailed from Senegal, where he's studying," I said. The soldier grunted and stepped into the hall to continue reading my private letters.

I sorted through some of the other papers on the floor, and I couldn't believe what I saw. There, in one big envelope, was my high school diploma, my university progress report, and nearly $30 of my scholarship money that I'd tucked away. Suddenly I was rich . . . and could prove that I was educated!

I left campus right away and used one of my American dollars to pay for a taxi back to Kigali, thanking God all the way home for answering yet another prayer. He truly was keeping His promise and watching over me like His own daughter.

A few shops had reopened in the city, and I bought some secondhand clothes, new shoes, perfume, and deodorant. Then I had my hair done for the first time in five months. I went home feeling like a lady again. Aloise almost had a heart attack when she saw me emerge from my room, dressed up and looking beautiful.

"Whatever it is you pray for, pray I get some, too," she said, laughing her big-hearted guffaw. She laughed even harder when I showed her all the groceries I'd bought with the money I had left over—enough to last us another month!

THE NEXT MORNING I HEADED OFF TO THE UN to resume my job hunt. I looked good, I smelled good, I had my diploma, and I felt fit and confident—I was a young career woman ready to take her place in the world.

The Ghanaian security guard didn't question me at the gate this time; in fact, I don't think he even recognized me because he buzzed me in without question, smiling as I passed. As soon as I was in the building, I found my way to the personnel director's office and knocked on the door, interrupting the director in the middle of a conversation.

"How can I help you, miss?" he asked in French.

"I need a job, sir," I said in English . . . or at least I thought I did.

He looked confused. "Are you trying to say that you need a job?"

"Yes, sir, that's right—I need a job," I answered in French. It was obvious that my English was going to need some work.

"I see . . . wait here," he said, and disappeared into his office. A few minutes later his secretary came to talk to me and thoroughly looked me up and down. She was Rwandan, and for some reason disliked me instantly. "How did you get into the building? What are you looking for?" she asked in Kinyarwanda.

"I'm looking for a job."

"What experience do you have?"

"I've been to university, where I studied electronic engineering and math."

"The jobs here are secretarial—that is, when we have jobs. Can you use a computer or speak English?"

"I've never done secretarial work, but I have a little English."

"I see," she said brusquely. "Well, we don't have anything—maybe in three or four months. But with the skills you have, I doubt we'll find you anything. Please shut the door on your way out."

I was so upset when I left the office that I ran down the back stairs so no one would see me crying. Halfway down the steps a middle-aged gentleman called out to me in French: "Wait! Wait a minute, young lady! Can I talk to you?"

I wanted to keep running, but respect for my elders compelled me to answer. I quickly wiped away my tears. "Yes, sir?"

The man looked at me like he'd seen a ghost. "Um . . . um . . . I was wondering, why are you here?"

I worried that he was going to call security, yet I replied, "A job, sir . . . I'm looking for a job."

"Oh, have you seen the personnel director?"

The stairwell interrogation annoyed me, but again I answered out of respect. "Yes, sir, I saw him. But I was told that there are no jobs."

"Oh well, then." He scribbled something on a business card and handed it to me. "Show this at the gate tomorrow morning," he said. "I'll expect you in my office at 10 A.M. We'll see what we can do about getting you a job."

I didn't know what to say, so I just stared at the card as he continued up the stairs. It read:

Pierre Mehu

Spokesman, UNAMIR

United Nations Assistance Mission for Rwanda

I had no idea what a spokesman was, but it sounded important. And UNAMIR had been set up before the war to help bring a fairer government to Rwanda. Maybe I would be part of it!

When I met with Mr. Mehu the next morning, he told me that when he saw me on the stairs he'd mistaken me for a young Rwandan woman who'd worked for him before the war. He was very fond of her, and she'd been killed with her family during the genocide. He then asked me to tell him my story, which I did.

"What is your monthly income?" he asked.

"My what?"

"How much money do you earn in a month?"

"Nothing, zero. That's why I'm here."

"Well, we can't have that! I'm going to help you get a job. Your parents obviously did a good job raising you, and I want you to know that you'll only be an orphan if you want to be. From now on the UN will be a home for you, and you can talk to me like I'm your dad."

I smiled until it hurt—God truly was keeping His promise by sending angels to look out for me.

"You'll have to do all the tests, of course," Mr. Mehu continued, "but with your education, that shouldn't be a problem. How are your typing and English skills?"

"I can't really type, and I taught myself English while hiding in the bathroom."

"Well, then . . . sounds like you need a crash course."

Mr. Mehu introduced me to his secretary, Jeanne, and she spent the day showing me how to use the computer and write memos, along with the ins and outs of their filing system. I memorized every function of every button on the computer, and then I drew an exact replica of the keyboard on a piece of cardboard. I spent three days working on the computer, and stayed up three entire nights practicing, typing on my hand-drawn keyboard.

God must have been guiding my fingers, because on the fourth day I passed the UN typing test with a perfect score. A few days later I passed an English test and was declared qualified to work at the United Nations. I envisioned it, I dreamed it, I prayed for it, and now I had it!

Before I knew it, I was working as a clerk, and soon I was responsible for tracking all UN supplies coming into Rwanda from abroad—from new Jeeps to cargo containers of food. It was an important job, and I couldn't get over the fact that only a couple months earlier I'd been crouching in someone's tiny bathroom, not knowing if I'd live or die.

I was living proof of the power of prayer and positive thinking, which really are almost the same thing. God is the source of all positive energy, and prayer is the best way to tap in to His power.

God had brought me a long way from the bathroom, and He'd walked with me every step of the way: saving me from the killers; filling my heart with forgiveness; helping me learn English; delivering me to safety; providing me with friendship, shelter, and food; and finally, introducing me to Mr. Mehu and my dream job. No matter what I'd been through in the past several months, God had never left my side; I'd never been alone.

I LOVED MY NEW JOB; EACH DAY WAS MORE EXCITING THAN THE LAST. There were so many nationalities at the UN that I felt like a tourist in my own country. I was continually learning new skills, meeting new people, and honing my English.

And not only was I rich in God's blessings, but I was getting a paycheck, too! Soon I was able to send money to my aunts and buy food and new clothes for Aloise and her kids to thank them for all they'd done for me. They'd given me a home and a family when I needed one most . . . but I also knew that the time had come to leave.

By early October all my friends from the French camp had left Aloise's, and everything around me was starting to change. More than a million Tutsi refugees from the 1959 and 1973 genocides were returning to Rwanda from around the world, bringing children, grandchildren, and all manner of new cultural heritage and strange languages with them. They were changing the sound and look of the country. A million exiles returned, which was also the same number of Tutsis murdered in the genocide—a number beyond my comprehension.

As the Tutsis returned, more than two million Hutus fled Rwanda fearing vengeance killings. Most of them ended up living in squalid refugee camps in other countries, while many died of disease and malnutrition. There was suffering everywere. One day, when I'd learned more and saved enough money, I would leave the sadness of my country far behind me. But for now, I had small changes to make. Life in Rwanda was shifting, and I was shifting with it.

I asked God to find me a new home where I would be surrounded with love and positive feelings. This time He let me answer my own prayers when I opened up Aloise's front door. Standing on the doorstep, weeping with joy at having found me, was my dear friend and college roommate, Sarah. She'd managed to track me down, and we both screamed and threw our arms around each other. We spent hours catching up and shedding many tears. My heart broke all over again when I told her how the pastor had sent our brothers Augustine and Vianney out into the night—and how they'd died together. We cried for the boys we'd loved so much, and for the rest of my family—Sarah had known and loved them all.

"You will always have a family with us," Sarah said. "Come live at my house . . . we'll be sisters again!"

Sarah was so special to me, and her offer so generous and inviting, that I accepted on the spot. I packed my things and moved into her parents' house that very day. Aloise didn't mind too much since Sarah's home was five minutes away, and I promised to visit her often.

I couldn't have asked for a more peaceful and loving home than Sarah's. Her elderly parents had been married 55 years, but they still teased and cherished each other like teenagers. They were devout Christians, went to church every morning, and prayed together every evening. It was the perfect place for me to reestablish my close personal connection with God . . . and the perfect place for me to mourn my family and begin to heal.

At Sarah's, my wounded heart slowly became strong enough for me to put the words I still could barely speak down on paper. The time had come for me to write my brother Aimable, who was still in Senegal and didn't even know I was alive. I'd put off this painful task, partly because there had been no mail service, but more in the hopes that if I didn't see the words, then the painful events hadn't really happened. But they *did* happen—they were real, and I was finally beginning to accept it.

I placed my father's rosary on the table beside me and began to write: *My dearest Aimable, this is the saddest letter I have ever written, the saddest letter you will ever receive. . . .*

>—<

CHAPTER 23

Burying the Dead

"Where are your parents living?" This question was put to me a few months after I'd started my job at the United Nations.

"They're not living, except in my heart," I answered patiently. "They were killed in the genocide."

The UN was not the easiest place to ignore my sorrow. Most of the people working there were from outside the country, and when they learned about the fate of my family, they were very curious about how I'd survived when the vast majority of my tribespeople had been murdered.

"I'm so sorry," the person speaking to me said now. "I didn't know. I hope I haven't upset you." His name was Colonel Gueye, and he was a Senegalese officer responsible for a number of the UN peacekeepers who'd come to Rwanda to help stabilize the county.

I told the colonel not to worry about upsetting me. After all I'd been through, questions were the least of my worries. I let him know that I still had aunts and an uncle living in my home province of Kibuye, although I hadn't seen them since the war.

"Ah, Kibuye . . . I have quite a few soldiers stationed there," he said. "If you ever want to visit your relatives, I'd be happy to give you a lift and escort you myself. You can even bring a friend."

It was a great offer, as travel around the country was still difficult and unsafe.

"Really? You just tell me when, and I'll be ready, Colonel."

Two weeks later Sarah and I were strapped into a helicopter and soaring above the green hills of Rwanda, holding each other's hands and giggling with wild excitement. Neither of us had ever flown before, so we had no idea that when the colonel offered to give us a lift, he'd meant it literally!

Looking down at my beautiful country, it was hard to believe the ugly truth of the genocide. How many times had I wished during those dark days that I'd been born a bird? How many times had I dreamed about flying away from my bathroom cell and above the relentless horror? And now here I was, flying back to visit the scene of the crime. It had taken a lifetime for me to escape from Mataba and get to Kigali—and it took only 30 minutes to return.

I wished that Aimable could have been with me, but it was impossible. The mail was still slow, and it had taken me weeks to finally get a return letter from him. He'd written that he was so happy to hear from me that he couldn't find words to express his emotions. He'd watched the news reports during the genocide and had resigned himself to the fact that our entire family had perished, along with almost every other Tutsi in Rwanda. There was no way he could have returned to the country during the holocaust without being murdered himself.

Unfortunately, he just couldn't afford to come home at the moment. He was a student, had no income, and lived 3,000 miles away in Senegal. The airfare alone would cost 2,000 American dollars, which was an unimaginable sum! The European organization that was funding his scholarship refused to pay for him to travel to Rwanda, saying that it was still a war zone and far too dangerous. My brother wanted to quit school and come live with me, but I told him that the best way for him to honor Mom and Dad was to finish his studies with top marks. We agreed to write each other every week and put money aside for a future visit. And now, thanks to the free lift to Mataba, I'd be visiting our old home without my only remaining brother.

AFTER THE HELICOPTER LANDED, COLONEL GUEYE LEFT US at the soldiers' camp in the capable hands of a young captain named Traore, who introduced us to everyone as Colonel Gueye's daughters. Unlike my earlier stays in military compounds, here Sarah and I had our own room, beds to sleep in, delicious food, and the respect and goodwill of each and every soldier. We even sat up with them until the wee hours as they sang traditional Senegalese songs and shared jokes with each other. Sarah felt welcome and safe, and I was happy that I'd come home.

The next day we were preparing to leave for the five-mile hike to my village, when Captain Traore expressed concern about our safety. The genocide was over, but a palpable current of hostility ran through the country, and killing was still commonplace. The captain insisted on sending us with an armed escort—which consisted of no less than two dozen soldiers and five armored vehicles. We wouldn't be slinking into Mataba as returning refugees; instead, we'd enter with the pride of warriors. I had cowered too long in that village, and it felt good to go back with my head held high.

My mood quickly dissolved into morbid sadness as we drove beneath the familiar sky of my childhood. I began weeping as we turned onto the road where my brothers and I had walked so often, then passed my mom's now-deserted schoolhouse, and rolled by the path we'd followed my dad along to go for our morning swims in Lake Kivu.

Sarah put her arm around my shoulders to console me, but it was no good—I was inconsolable. I also saw shadowy faces peering at us through shuttered windows and closed gates . . . faces that belonged to the extremist Hutus who'd hunted and killed so many of my people. They owned the only houses still standing after they themselves had burned most of the Tutsi homes.

And then we reached my family's house.

It was completely destroyed: no roof, no windows, no doors. A few partial walls stood watch over the scorched earth where we'd spent days listening to the radio while the killers prepared their massacre. I wandered through the stone skeleton, visiting the vacant rooms that had once formed my parents' dream home. There were no remnants of destroyed furniture or burnt clothing—our belongings had obviously been pilfered before the house was torched.

Several of my surviving Tutsi neighbors saw our military escort and came out to greet me. They informed me of the grim events that had transpired while I was in hiding, telling me how my mother had been murdered and where her remains had been buried.

Some of Damascene's friends took me to the shallow grave where they'd hastily buried what was left of him. Karubu, our housekeeper, had witnessed my beloved brother's execution and gave me a word-for-word, blow-by-blow account.

The heartrending memories and the gory, gruesome details were all too much for me. I'd just begun to heal, and now I felt my wounds forced open again by the onslaught of brutal reality. I wanted to ask my neighbors and the soldiers to help me give my mother and brother a proper burial, but I couldn't speak. The lump growing in my throat stopped my voice, so I waved for the soldiers to take me back to the camp.

As we drove away from my home, past the unmarked mounds of dirt that covered Mother and Damascene, I felt the bitter, dirty taste of hatred in my mouth. On the return trip I looked at the faces peering at us as we passed, and I knew with all my heart that those people had blood on their hands—their neighbors' blood . . . *my family's* blood. I wanted the soldiers to douse Mataba in gasoline and let me light the match that would reduce it to ashes.

I went straight to bed when we arrived at the camp without talking to anyone. My soul was at war with itself. I'd struggled so hard to forgive but now felt duped for having done so; I had no clemency left in me. Seeing my home in ruins and visiting the lonely, forgotten graves of my loved ones had choked the life out of my forgiving spirit. When my neighbors whispered the stories of my family's sadistic murders in my ear, the feelings of hatred that I thought I'd banished from my soul sprang violently from the depths of my being with renewed vigor. My heart hungered for revenge, and I raged inside myself. *Those bloody animals! They are animals, animals, animals!*

I tossed and turned for hours. I knew the devil was tempting me—that he was leading me away from the light of God, from the freedom of His forgiveness. I could feel the weight of my negative thoughts dragging me away from the one light that had guided me through the darkness. I never felt lonelier than I did that night. God was my truest friend, and these feelings were a wall between us. I knew that my thoughts caused Him pain, and that knowledge tortured me.

I rolled out of bed and got down on my knees. "Forgive my evil thoughts, God," I prayed. "Please . . . as You always have, take this pain from me and cleanse my heart. Fill me with the power of Your love and forgiveness. Those who did these horrible things are still Your children, so let me help them, and help me to forgive them. Oh, God, help me to *love* them."

A sudden rush of air flooded my lungs. I heaved a heavy sigh of relief, and my head dropped back on the pillow. I was at peace again. Yes, I was sad—deeply sad—but my sadness felt good. I let it embrace me and found that it was clean, with no tinge of bitterness or hatred. I missed my family desperately, but the anger that had gripped me like a returning malignancy was gone.

The people who'd hurt my family had hurt themselves even more, and they deserved my pity. There was no doubt that they had to be punished for their crimes against humanity and against God. There was already talk at the UN about creating an international tribunal to capture those responsible, and I prayed that it would happen. But I prayed for compassion as well. I asked God for the forgiveness that would end the cycle of hatred—hatred that was always dangerously close to the surface.

I knew that my heart and mind would always be tempted to feel anger—to find blame and hate. But I resolved that when the negative feelings came upon me, I wouldn't wait for them to grow or fester. I would always turn immediately to the Source of all true power: I would turn to God and let His love and forgiveness protect and save me.

When I lifted my head, I noticed that the moon was already up. I heard the soldiers laughing and playing music, so I went outside. Sarah and I smiled at each other, and then I smiled at everyone there. The soldiers were having a party, and they were surprised to see me join them looking so happy. They danced all night, as Sarah and I watched and cheered them on.

THE NEXT DAY I ASKED THE CAPTAIN IF HE'D TAKE ME BACK to the village so that I could properly lay my mother and brother to rest. He was concerned about my reaction the day before and asked if I were strong enough. I assured him that I was, and he provided me with the same military escort to the village.

On the way, we stopped to see my aunts Jeanne and Esperance, who were living close to my old house. I hadn't seen them since they'd left the French camp. Neither had fully recovered from their ordeal and probably never would, but at least they were in much better condition now. We had an emotional roadside reunion, but I kept my heart in check to prepare for the solemn duty ahead. I told them to find anyone who wanted to say good-bye to Mom and Damascene and meet me at my old home.

Most of the Tutsi genocide survivors in my village turned out, and a few Hutu chums joined us as well. One old family friend, Kayitare, brought two coffins with him; someone else brought a shovel and a Bible; and we all went together to recover the remains. First we dug for Damascene; some neighbors crowded around me to block my view, gently pushing me back to protect me from seeing what was left of him.

I shoved past them. "He's my brother—I *have* to see him," I insisted. I don't think I could ever have accepted that Damascene was really dead if I couldn't see his body with my own eyes. Then I heard the shovel scrape against bone, and I saw him . . . I saw his rib cage. The first thing I noticed was that he had no clothes on, and I remembered how they'd tried to strip him of his dignity before executing him.

"Don't look," Esperance said. But I had to—I saw his rib cage but nothing else. They'd chopped him up—his arms, his head. . . . *Oh, God, my sweet Damascene, what did they do to you?* I let out a kind of animal whimper.

Someone bent down to the grave, then stood up and turned to me, holding my brother's skull in his hand. The jawbone was protruding, and then I saw the teeth . . . I recognized the teeth. All that remained of his beautiful smile was right there, staring up at me in a twisted, grotesque grin.

"Oh no . . . oh, Damascene . . . oh, blessed Mary, Mother of God!" The earth rushed up at me, my head hit a stone, and then there was only blackness.

I hadn't expected to faint, but when my mind at long last acknowledged my brother's death, it felt as if all the oxygen had been sucked out of the world. My relatives and neighbors revived me and lifted me to my feet, and we put Damascene's remains into a coffin and took it with us to find Mom. This time they insisted that I not look at the body, saying it was too decomposed and would be too upsetting. I acquiesced because I'd reached the limit of my pain. No matter how much I steeled my heart, the sight of my mother like that would have been too much for my loving eyes to bear. I agreed to bury her remains without seeing them. Instead, I'd remember her as she'd been in life . . . as she would forever stay in my heart and in my dreams.

As someone pounded nails into the lid of my mother's coffin, I looked at the faces of my friends and relatives—shattered faces reflecting shattered lives. There was my cousin, who'd been forced to watch her three boys slaughtered in front of her; my once-iron-willed Uncle Paul, who was now reduced to a shadow of his former self by the deaths of his beloved wife and seven children; and my aunts, whose husbands were dead and whose children were ill beyond recovery.

We all shared in the misery that had descended upon the village, but I knew that the people gathered around me had lost much more than I had. They'd lost their faith—and in doing so, they'd also lost hope. I stared at the coffins of my mother and Damascene and thought of my father and Vianney, whose bodies I would never recover . . . and I thanked God. I may have lost everything, but I'd kept my faith, and it made me strong. It also comforted me and let me know that life still held purpose.

"Where shall we put them? Where shall we bury them?" Uncle Paul asked, sobbing as he ran his hands along the crude pine caskets.

"Home," I said. "We'll take them home and lay them to rest."

We carried the bodies of my mother and brother into the ruins of our home and dug a large grave in the center of one of the rooms where laughter and love had once echoed. There were no priests left in the village, so we performed the burial rites ourselves. We sang some of my mother's favorite hymns and prayed many prayers. I asked God to hold my family close to Him and watch over their beautiful souls in heaven . . . and then I said good-bye.

"It's time to go home, Sarah—time to go back to Kigali," I whispered to my sweet friend, my adopted sister who had taken me in and given me a new family.

Soon we were in the clouds again, flying high above my village, high above the sorrows that had stained our lives . . . so high that I felt I could touch the face of God.

≫≪

CHAPTER 24

Forgiving the Living

I knew that my family was at peace, but that didn't ease the pain of missing them. And I couldn't shake the crippling sorrow that seized my heart whenever I envisioned how they'd been killed. Every night I prayed to be released from my private agony, from the nightmares that haunted my sleep and troubled my days. It took a while, but as always, God answered my prayers. This time, He did so by sending me a dream unlike any I've ever had.

I was in a helicopter flying over my family's house, but I was trapped in a dark cloud. I could see Mom, Dad, Damascene, and Vianney high above me, standing in the sky and bathed in a warm, white light that radiated tranquility. The light intensified and spread across the sky until it engulfed the dark cloud hiding me. And suddenly, I was with my family again. The dream was so real that I reached out and felt the warmth of their skin, the gentleness of their touch. I was so happy that I danced in the air.

Damascene was wearing a crisp white shirt and blue trousers. He looked at me with a joyful glow and gave me his brilliant smile. My mother, father, and Vianney stood behind him, holding hands and beaming at me. "Hey, Immaculée, it's good to see that we can still make you happy," my beautiful brother said. "You've been gloomy far too long and must stop all this crying. Look at the wonderful place we're in . . . can you see how happy we are? If you continue to believe that we're suffering, you'll force us to return to the pain we've left behind. I know how much you miss us, but do you really want us to come back and suffer?"

"No, no, Damascene!" I cried out, as tears of joy poured from my eyes. "Don't come back here! Wait for me there, and I will come join you all. When God is done with me in this life, I will come to you."

"We'll be here waiting, dear sister. Now heal your heart. You must love, and you must forgive those who have trespassed against us."

My family slowly receded into the sky until they disappeared into the heavens. I was still hovering over my house, but I was no longer in a dark cloud . . . and no longer in a helicopter. I was flying like a bird above my village, above the pastor's house and the French camp, above all the forests and rivers and waterfalls of my beautiful country—I was soaring above Rwanda.

I felt so liberated from grief and gravity that I began to sing for joy. I sang from my heart, the words tumbling happily from my mouth. The song was "Mwami Shimirwa," which in Kinyarwanda means "Thank You, God, for love that is beyond our understanding."

My singing woke the entire house, since it was the middle of the night. Sarah's mom came running into my room, worried that I'd fallen ill and was delirious with fever.

From that night onward, my tears began to dry and my pain eased. I never again agonized over the fate of my family. I accepted that I would always mourn and miss them, but I'd never spend another moment worrying about the misery they'd endured. By sending me that dream, God had shown me that my family was in a place beyond suffering.

He'd also shown me that I had to make another trip to my village.

A FEW WEEKS LATER COLONEL GUEYE GAVE ME ANOTHER lift home, but this time we drove cross-country. The landscape of my youth no longer saddened me; rather, I was heartened by the warm memories stirred by the sights and sounds around me. I wandered with friends through my mother's banana plantation and my father's mountainside coffee crops. I told my aunts that if they weren't afraid of going outside, they could harvest the crops to support themselves.

Aunt Jeanne told me not to worry about her being afraid: She was getting a gun and would learn how to shoot. "Next time I'll be ready," she said.

Next time, I thought with a heavy sigh.

I went to my old house to visit my mom and Damascene. I knelt by their graves and told them all that had happened since I'd last seen them. I told them about my job at the UN and what I planned to do in the future. I missed seeing their faces and hearing their voices, and I wept. But this time, my tears were a release, not a sorrow.

And then it was time to do what I'd come to do.

I ARRIVED AT THE PRISON LATE IN THE AFTERNOON and was greeted by Semana, the new burgomaster of Kibuye. Semana had been a teacher before the genocide, as well as a colleague and good friend of my dad's—he was like an uncle to me. Four of his six children had been killed in the slaughter, and I told him he must have faith that his little ones were with God.

"I can see how much the world has changed; the children now comfort the parents," he replied sadly.

As burgomaster, Semana was a powerful politician in charge of arresting and detaining the killers who had terrorized our area. He'd interrogated hundreds of Interahamwe and knew better than anyone which killers had murdered whom.

And he knew why I'd come to see him. "Do you want to meet the leader of the gang that killed your mother and Damascene?"

"Yes, sir, I do."

I watched through Semana's office window as he crossed a court yard to the prison cell and then returned, shoving a disheveled, limping old man in front of him. I jumped up with a start as they approached, recognizing the man instantly. His name was Felicien, and he was a successful Hutu businessman whose children I'd played with in primary school. He'd been a tall, handsome man who always wore expensive suits and had impeccable manners. I shivered, remembering that it had been his voice I'd heard calling out my name when the killers searched for me at the pastor's. Felicien had hunted me.

Semana pushed Felicien into the office, and he stumbled onto his knees. When he looked up from the floor and saw that I was the one who was waiting for him, the color drained from his face. He quickly shifted his gaze and stared at the floor.

"Stand up, killer!" Semana shouted. "Stand up and explain to this girl why her family is dead. Explain to her why you murdered her mother and butchered her brother. Get up, I said! Get up and tell her!" Semana screamed even louder, but the battered man remained hunched and kneeling, too embarrassed to stand and face me.

His dirty clothing hung from his emaciated frame in tatters. His skin was sallow, bruised, and broken; and his eyes were filmed and crusted. His once handsome face was hidden beneath a filthy, matted beard; and his bare feet were covered in open, running sores.

I wept at the sight of his suffering. Felicien had let the devil enter his heart, and the evil had ruined his life like a cancer in his soul. He was now the victim of his victims, destined to live in torment and regret. I was overwhelmed with pity for the man.

"He looted your parents' home and robbed your family's plantation, Immaculée. We found your dad's farm machinery at his house, didn't we?" Semana yelled at Felicien. "After he killed Rose and Damascene, he kept looking for you . . . he wanted you dead so he could take over your property. Didn't you, pig?" Semana shouted again.

I flinched, letting out an involuntary gasp. Semana looked at me, stunned by my reaction and confused by the tears streaming down my face. He grabbed Felicien by the shirt collar and hauled him to his feet. "What do you have to say to her? What do you have to say to Immaculée?"

Felicien was sobbing. I could feel his shame. He looked up at me for only a moment, but our eyes met. I reached out, touched his hands lightly, and quietly said what I'd come to say.

"I forgive you."

My heart eased immediately, and I saw the tension release in Felicien's shoulders before Semana pushed him out the door and into the courtyard. Two soldiers yanked Felicien up by his armpits and dragged him back toward his cell. When Semana returned, he was furious.

"What was that all about, Immaculée? That was the man who murdered your family. I brought him to you to question . . . to spit on if you wanted to. But you forgave him! How could you do that? Why did you forgive him?"

I answered him with the truth: "Forgiveness is all I have to offer."

>>-<<

EPILOGUE

New Love, New Life

It's impossible to predict how long it will take a broken heart to heal. I was blessed, though: With God's help, my heart was strong enough to love another after two years. But while I healed, I lived a quiet, reflective life.

I continued to work at the UN and live with Sarah's family, and during my free time I volunteered at a Kigali orphanage, acting as a big sister to dozens of traumatized, lonely children. I was always on the lookout for the brothers I'd cared for at the French camp—I never found them, but I did find plenty of other youngsters in need of love.

In late 1995, I was finally reunited with Aimable. His scholarship administrators decided that Rwanda was stable enough to travel to and paid for his ticket home. We'd written often and talked on the phone a few times during the year, but we weren't prepared for actually seeing each other face-to-face. I'll never forget our meeting at the airport. Rather than a huge outpouring of emotion, our reunion was tentative, as if we were guarding our hearts. We hugged and kissed, but cautiously, for I was afraid of his pain and he of mine. We found it difficult to look each other in the eye, knowing that if our true feelings surfaced, we'd be unable to control them—that if we began crying, we'd never be able to stop.

My brother and I went to a restaurant with some friends of mine and playacted our way through dinner, talking about his studies and my job, and even laughing at my friends' jokes. But later that night, when I was alone in my bed, I cried my eyes out. I'm sure he did, too.

The next day it was easier for us to be together. We loved each other so much that we found comfort in each other's company, even though seeing each other was a painful reminder of our family's tragedy. I wanted to tell him that I was strong enough to deal with the pain, and I wanted to console him, but I knew instinctively that he was inconsolable. After a while, it was clear that we'd silently agreed not to talk about what had happened to our family. We mentioned everyone by name, but spoke about them as if they were still alive—it was the only way we could cope. We carried on like that through letters and phone calls for the next two years. And things didn't change when Aimable graduated as a doctor of veterinary medicine and moved to Kigali. We saw each other every day but would mention the genocide in very general terms, as if it had happened to someone else. When he went to visit the graves of Mom and Damascene in Mataba, he didn't ask me to go with him.

It's been that way for us ever since. Aimable still lives in Kigali, is a successful doctor, and has a lovely wife and child. We love each other dearly and are as close as ever, speaking often and writing at least once a week. But still, after more than a decade, we never talk about our family in the past tense. I suppose it's our way of keeping their memory alive.

I PASSED MANY EVENINGS CLOISTERED IN PRAYER and meditation at a nearby Jesuit center, which became a second home to me. It was in those quiet surroundings that I was again able to experience the strong, intimate connection with God that had saved me during my long months in hiding.

As my heart slowly recovered, I began to dream of sharing my life with someone special, of having a family of my own to care for and love. But I was nervous . . . I remembered my experience with John and was unwilling to subject my fragile heart to a relationship that could go nowhere and end painfully. So, as I'd learned to do whenever faced with a problem or challenge, I called on God. If I wanted a marriage made in heaven, what better matchmaker could there be?

The Bible tells us that if we ask, we shall receive, and that's exactly what I did: I asked God to bring me the man of my dreams. I didn't want to cheat myself—I wanted to be very clear on the kind of person God should send me. So I sat down with a piece of paper and sketched the face of the person I wanted to marry, and then I listed his height and other physical features. I asked for a man of strong character, one who had a warm personality; who was kind, loving, and tender; had a sense of humor and strong morals; who loved me for who I was; who enjoyed children as much as I did; and, above all, who loved God.

I didn't want to give God a deadline, but having placed no restrictions on race, nationality, or color—and considering that there were more than five billion people on the planet—I figured that six months would be a reasonable amount of time to wait for the Lord to send me my soul mate. I did include one caveat: Because I loved the rosary and the Virgin Mary so much, and so many other aspects of Catholicism were important to me, I told God that He had better send a Catholic. I wanted to make sure that there would be no tension in my marriage because of religion, and that my husband worshiped God in the same way I did.

Once I was clear on exactly what I wanted, I began to visualize it, believing in my heart that it had already come to pass. I'd put it all in God's hands and knew that it was only a matter of time before He would bless me with my wish. But to hurry things along, I took out my father's red and white rosary and began praying for my husband to show up. Three months later, he did: Mr. Bryan Black, who was sent by God, courtesy of the UN, all the way from America!

Ironically, Bryan came to the country to help set up the International Criminal Tribunal for Rwanda, the UN court prosecuting those responsible for planning the genocide. Bryan had worked for the UN for many years and was excited to be part of a mission that would bring justice to the killers. Personally, I felt that he was on a mission from God.

When I first saw Bryan at UN headquarters, I thought that he looked exactly like the man I'd asked God to send me. Later, when I passed him in the hall and saw the deep gentleness in his eyes, I was sure that he was "the one." But since I'd put my faith in God, I waited for Him to bring Bryan to me . . . and He did.

Bryan asked me out on a date, and we had a wonderful time. At the end of the evening, I was certain that we were a perfect match and that he was the person I'd spend the rest of my life with . . . if only he were Catholic! I braced myself, and asked him the big question: "What religion are you?"

"I'm Catholic."

I wanted to jump into his arms and shout, "Praise God! Welcome to my life—you're here to stay!" But I worried that I'd scare the poor guy off. So instead, I took his hand in mine, smiled, and said, "Me, too."

I never burdened Bryan with the full story of what I'd been through during the genocide, but he listened to me whenever my heart was heavy, and he let me cry on his shoulder whenever I felt the need.

TWO YEARS LATER BRYAN AND I WERE MARRIED IN A TRADITIONAL Rwandan ceremony, and we came to America a short while later, in 1998. We have a loving, supportive marriage, and God has blessed us with two beautiful children: our daughter, Nikeisha, and our son, Bryan, Jr. Every morning when I wake up to my two little angels, I can see the beauty and power of God in their faces. I never stop thanking Him for all His precious gifts.

God remains part of my life every day and in every way; He sustains me, protects me, and fulfills me. He makes me a better wife, a better mother, and a better person. And He's helped me make a career for myself as well. After my children were born, I wanted to resume my working life, but finding a good job in New York City was even more challenging than it had been in Kigali after the genocide—there were so many people, and so few jobs!

But I prayed for God to guide me, and then I looked for the position I wanted—at the United Nations in Manhattan. Once I knew where I wanted to work, I visualized that I already had a job there, using the same technique of positive thinking I'd always used: believe and receive! I went to the UN Website, printed out the directory that listed the employees' names and titles, and then added my name to the list. I even gave myself a telephone extension! I tacked the directory onto my wall and looked at it every day. Of course, I also filled out an application, submitted a résumé, and made follow-up phone calls—but so had more than a thousand other people. I kept looking at my directory, believing that the job was mine, and I prayed every day until my phone rang. Sure enough, I was short-listed out of hundreds of other applicants and was offered the job after I went in for an interview. I've never ceased to be amazed by seeing God's power at work!

This is the same power that I feel propelling me forward into the next phase of my life. God saved my soul and spared my life for a reason: He left me to tell my story to others and show as many people as possible the healing power of His love and forgiveness.

There are people I left behind that I must help. I hope to return to Rwanda as often as I can to aid in restoring hope to the hearts of genocide survivors, especially the orphaned children. I am currently setting up a foundation that will help victims of genocide and war everywhere to heal in body, mind, and spirit.

GOD'S MESSAGE EXTENDS BEYOND BORDERS: Anyone in the world can learn to forgive those who have injured them, however great or small that injury may be. I see the truth of this every day. For example, I recently shared my story with a new friend, and a few days later she called to say that my experiences had inspired her to contact an uncle she'd once been close to but hadn't spoken to in years.

"We'd had a big fight, and I was so angry that I swore I'd never speak to him again," she confided. "But after hearing how you managed to forgive the people who killed your family, I had to pick up the phone and call him. I didn't ask him for an apology—I just opened my heart and forgave him. Soon we were talking the way we used to, with so much love. We couldn't believe that we'd wasted so many years."

Similarly, a genocide survivor whose family had been murdered called me from Rwanda not long ago, crying over the phone and asking me to explain the steps I'd taken to forgive the killers.

"I thought you were crazy to forgive them, Immaculée—that you were letting them off the hook. But the pain and bitterness I've been carrying in my heart for 11 years is about to kill me. I've been so miserable for so long that I don't have the energy to live anymore. But I keep hearing people talk about how you forgave your family's killers and moved on with your life . . . that you're happy and have a husband, children, and a career! I need to learn how to let go of my hatred, too. I need to live again."

I told her how I put my trust in God, and related all I'd done to forgive and move ahead . . . everything I've now written down in this book. She thanked me and later told me that she'd asked God to help her forgive the killers, too.

Then there was the woman in Atlanta who approached me in tears at the end of a talk I gave. She told me that her parents had been killed in the Nazi Holocaust when she was a baby: "My heart has been full of anger my entire life . . . I've suffered and cried over my parents for so many years. But hearing your story about what you lived through and were able to forgive has inspired me. I've been try-ing all my life to forgive the people who killed my parents, and now I think I can do it. I can let go of my anger and be happy."

At the same seminar, a 92-year-old lady put her arms around me and hugged me tightly. She was so emotional that she was barely able to speak, but she found her voice. I'll never forget her words: "I thought it was too late for me to forgive. I've been waiting to hear someone say what you did—I had to know that it was possible to for-give the unforgivable. I am at peace now."

As for the land of my birth, I know that Rwanda can heal herself if each heart learns the lesson of forgiveness. Tens of thousands who were jailed for killing during the genocide are starting to be released into their old towns and villages, so if there was ever a time for for-giveness, it is now. Rwanda can be a paradise again, but it will take the love of the entire world to heal my homeland. And that's as it should be, for what happened in Rwanda happened to us all—humanity was wounded by the genocide.

The love of a single heart can make a world of difference. I believe that we can heal Rwanda—and our world—by healing one heart at a time.

I hope my story helps.

>—«

ACKNOWLEDGMENTS

First, I must thank God above all others for being a wonderful father and best friend, my truest confidant . . . and my savior. You have been my constant companion in the best of times and the very, very worst of times. Thank You, God, for opening my heart and letting me love again. I am nothing without You, and I am everything with You. I surrender to You, Lord—let Your will be done in my life. I continue to walk in Your footsteps.

To the Holy Mother, the Blessed Virgin Mary: I feel you with me always. Words can't convey the depth of my gratitude for your love and care. Keep my heart close to yours, Mother—you make me whole, and I will love you forever. Thank you for appearing in Kibeho to warn us of the danger ahead . . . if only we'd listened to you!

To Dr. Wayne Dyer: You are an angel sent from heaven. I thank God for bringing you into my life, and I feel as if our spirits have known each other forever! Your unsurpassed kindness, sage advice, and fatherly affection mean the world to me. It's so easy to understand why so many people have been inspired by your words—you are my hero, and I love you dearly. Thank you from the bottom of my heart for believing in me, for guiding me toward my dream, and for making me aware of my true calling. And thank you for making this book a reality and letting me tell my story.

To Skye Dyer: Thank you for introducing me to your dad. I love you!

To Maya Labos: I love traveling with you—thank you for all your support and kindness. I'm so glad I know you, and I love you!

To Reid Tracy: A thousand thanks for believing in me and making all of this happen, for standing behind me all the way, and for making Hay House a home for my book.

To the wonderful team at Hay House: Jill Kramer, Shannon Littrell, Nancy Levin, Christy Salinas, Jacqui Clark, Stacey Smith, and Jeannie Liberati—you have been a joy to work with. Thank you all for your guidance, patience, and encouragement.

To my collaborator, Steve Erwin: After working together on this book, I don't think that anyone knows me as well as you do. You are a wonderful person, and like a brother to me now. Thank you for being such a good therapist—the sensitivity you showed when asking so many intimate questions about my family means so much to me. I thank God for your magic hands—your writing brought my words and emotions to life. My gratitude to your wife, Natasha, as well, who understands all the emotions I expressed in this book, since we share the pain of losing our moms too soon. Natasha, you're like a sister!

To Judith Garten: I love you. Thank you for encouraging me and believing in the message of this book.

To Gail Straub and David Gershon: Thank you for pushing me to finish writing my story and for making me believe in myself.

To Ned Leavitt: I thank you with all my heart for your wonderful advice and believing that I had something important to say.

To Elizabeth Lesser: Thank you for the good counsel and for inviting me to the Omega workshop in New York where I met Wayne.

To Vincent Kayijuka and Esperance Fundira: I'll never forget how you encouraged and believed in me from the beginning. I love you guys! And a big thanks to Wariara Mbuga, Robert McMahon, Lila Ramos, Anne Kellett, Bill Berkeley, and Rebeka Martensen for all the help, kind words, good advice, and invaluable encouragement.

Many thanks to my colleagues at UNDP and the Evaluation Office—with a special thanks to David Rider Smith, Ruth Abraham, and Anish Pradhan, for your understanding and support. God bless you—I love you.

To the many dear friends I couldn't mention, yet who have helped me in one way or another: Thank you—you are all in my heart.

And a very special thanks to two very special priests, Father Ganza Jean Baptiste and my godfather, Father Jean Baptiste Bugingo.

To my brother Aimable Ntukanyagwe, with whom I share so many memories of love and sorrow, and so much unspoken pain: I hope that in *Left to Tell,* you'll find answers to many of the questions you've been unable to ask, and I've been unable to offer. I thank the Almighty that you are alive—you mean the world to me. Don't worry about our folks . . . they're happy, and they are our special advocates in heaven! Thank you for being such a wonderful big brother—for the unfailing love you've shown me from my earliest memory, for your faith in me, and for always encouraging me to write our family story. And my warmest thanks to Sauda: I'm blessed to be able to call you my sister-in-law and my friend—thank you for extending our family. As a fellow genocide survivor, this book will have special meaning for you. I love you so much!

To Chantal Nyirarukundo, Consolee Nishimwe, and Stella Umutoni: You are my little sisters! Thank you for being excited about this book—you've been a great inspiration. Know that it is for you as well, for surviving.

To my beautiful children, Nikeisha and B.J. (Bryan Jr.), and my little nephew, Ryan: You are my heart, my little angels who came to me like flowers from God. Thank you for the purity of your love and for giving me a reason to live again. I wish that we lived in a world where your innocent lives weren't affected by hatred and you'd never have to hear the words *genocide* or *holocaust*. When you're old enough, you will meet your grandparents and uncles in the pages of *Left to Tell*—their memories will live on in my book. But for now I will pass along their love to you whenever you wrap your precious arms around me for hugs. You are my life, and I love you.

And finally, but certainly not least, thank you to my wonderful husband, Bryan: You rescued me from loneliness and are truly my better half—the half sent by God to complete me. Thank you for your tireless efforts and for helping me tell my story, and for all your encouragement and the late nights of reading and editing. Thank you for your constant love and protection, and for accepting God as our friend. I love you, sweetheart, with all my heart and soul.

— **Immaculée**

Immaculée, thank you for letting me help you tell your remarkable story to the world. Your courage, faith, resilience, insight, and wisdom continue to move and inspire me. Working with you has been my privilege, and I'm blessed to be able to call you my friend.

Thanks to Jill Kramer at Hay House for this opportunity—and for your professionalism, courtesy, and speed-of-light e-mails.

Thanks also to Shannon Littrell at Hay House for your excellent suggestions and comments.

A special thanks to Faith Farthing of FinalEyes Communications for your sound advice and exacting attention to detail.

And most of all, thank you to Natasha Stoynoff, my wife, my life, my everything. God only knows where I'd be without you.

— **Steve Erwin**

ABOUT THE AUTHORS

Immaculée Ilibagiza

Immaculée Ilibagiza was born in Rwanda and studied electronic and mechanical engineering at the National University. She lost most of her family during the 1994 genocide. Four years later, she emigrated from Rwanda to the United States and began working for the United Nations in New York City. She is establishing the Ilibagiza Foundation to help others heal from the long-term effects of genocide and war. Immaculée lives in Long Island with her husband, Bryan Black, and their two children, Nikeisha and Bryan, Jr.

Steve Erwin

Steve Erwin is a writer and award-winning journalist working in the print and broadcast media. Most recently, he was a foreign correspondent for the Canadian Broadcasting Corporation. He lives in Manhattan with his wife, journalist Natasha Stoynoff, and is writing his second novel.

Four Ways to Order!

1 ONLINE:
www.hayhouse.com

2 CALL:
800-654-5126

3 FAX ORDER FORM TO:
800-650-5115

4 MAIL ORDER FORM TO:
Left to Tell Wristbands
c/o Hay House, Inc., P.O. Box 5100,
Carlsbad, CA 92018-5100

NAME (please print)

ADDRESS

CITY   STATE   ZIP

DAYTIME PHONE (   )   EVENING PHONE (   )

We will call only if we have a question about your order.

SHIP TO (if different)

NAME (please print)

ADDRESS

CITY   STATE   ZIP

CUSTOMER IDENTIFICATION NUMBERS
Please print the numbers below as they
appear on your mailing label:

Priority Code:

Preferred
Customer #:

For your security, please provide the three- or four-digit code
from the signature line on your credit card.

Item#	Quantity	Description/Title	Amount

Subtotal	
CA Residents add 7.75% Tax	
Shipping	
Total	

HAY
HOUSE

※※

We hope you enjoyed this Hay House book. If you'd like to receive a free catalog featuring additional Hay House books and products, or if you'd like information about the Hay Foundation, please contact:

Hay House, Inc.
P.O. Box 5100
Carlsbad, CA 92018-5100

(760) 431-7695 or **(800) 654-5126**
(760) 431-6948 (fax) or **(800) 650-5115 (fax)**
www.hayhouse.com® • www.hayfoundation.org

※※

Published and distributed in Australia by: Hay House Australia Pty. Ltd. •
18/36 Ralph St. • Alexandria NSW 2015 • *Phone:* 612-9669-4299 •
Fax: 612-9669-4144 • www.hayhouse.com.au

Published and distributed in the United Kingdom by: Hay House UK, Ltd. •
Unit 62, Canalot Studios • 222 Kensal Rd., London W10 5BN •
Phone: 44-20-8962-1230 • *Fax:* 44-20-8962-1239 • www.hayhouse.co.uk

Published and distributed in the Republic of South Africa by:
Hay House SA (Pty), Ltd., P.O. Box 990, Witkoppen 2068 •
Phone/Fax: 27-11-706-6612 • orders@psdprom.co.za

Distributed in Canada by: Raincoast • 9050 Shaughnessy St.,
Vancouver, B.C. V6P 6E5 • *Phone:* (604) 323-7100 • *Fax:* (604) 323-2600

※※

Tune in to **www.hayhouseradio.com**™ for the best in inspirational talk radio featuring top Hay House authors! And, sign up via the Hay House USA Website to receive the Hay House online newsletter and stay informed about what's going on with your favorite authors. You'll receive bimonthly announcements about: Discounts and Offers, Special Events, Product Highlights, Free Excerpts, Giveaways, and more!
www.hayhouse.com®